Building a Successful Tennis Career

A practical guide on surviving and prospering as a teaching professional

Jack Thompson

TNY Books
Mc Cormick, SC

TNY Books
McCormick, SC

Published in the USA by TNY Books, 2022
Cover Design by TNY Media

Library of Congress Control Number: 2022915719

ISBN: 9798218039295 (Paperback)
ISBN: 9798218043797 (eBook)

Dedication

This book is dedicated to my wife, Pam, who is my soulmate and best friend; my daughters, Jacque and Ginny, my parents, John and Myrna, who taught me good character, self-reliance, independence, honesty, integrity and how to recover from failure; my sister Leigh and brother Larry; Dr. Bill Herbert, Dr. Don Sebolt and Dr. Craig Wrisberg, who gave me the educational background for my professional work; Dennis and Pat Van der Meer, who taught me how to be a quality pro, my friend and mentor, Pete Collins, who has been a source of knowledge, strength and inspiration for many years; John Raker, for his generosity and time in writing the foreword; Chad Reed – an excellent teaching pro, for his editorial input; Jake, Doris and Terri Smith, who gave me my first tennis job and taught me about business; Gray Cook, my partner and friend who rekindled my interest in strength training and conditioning; Don Regan; Dr. Allen Fox for his time and generosity in reviewing many of my articles and giving me good suggestions; Coach Ed Krass for making me a better college coach; Dr. David Staniford; Peggy Edwards (PTR) an exceptional editor, who has improved my writing and who gave me a chance to bring my articles to print; Dan Santorum, Julie Jilly, Steve Keller, Dr. Louie Cap and the entire staff at PTR for their ongoing hard work in improving tennis worldwide; all of the PTR International Master Professionals from whom I continue to learn; Mark Allen, Rena Goolsby, Tim Wilkison, Marvin Hedgepeth, Frank Eason and Jon Post for their editorial input; the many tennis pros who were so kind in giving their time for the interviews in this book; my students, past and present, who trust/have trusted me to help them; and to God who has helped me through the tough times and given me a love for my work.

Jack Thompson

In Memoriam

Virginia Wingfield Thompson

Jan. 29, 1988 - May 23, 2023

On Monday, May 23, 2022, our youngest daughter, (known to family and friends as "Ginny", "Gin Gin" or "Addie"), passed away suddenly and unexpectedly at our home in Salisbury, NC at just 34 years of age.

In her short time here, she was able to achieve what takes most people 7 to 8 decades to accomplish.

.Our love for her will always live on in our hearts and we hope that when we pass, we have done well enough to join her in heaven. Your friends and family will always love you Ginny!

Pamela Thompson, Jack Thompson, and
Jacque (Thompson) Jensen

"From what we get, we can make a living; what we give, however,
makes a life."

Arthur Ashe

"The difference between a successful person and others is not a lack of
strength, not a lack of knowledge, but rather a lack of will."

Vince Lombardi

"Don't aim for success if you want it; just do what you love and
believe in, and it will come naturally."

David Frost

"I think the teaching profession contributes more to the future of our
society than any other single profession."

John Wooden

"The art of teaching is the art of assisting discovery."

Mark Van Doren

Forward

I remember the moment I recognized that tennis career wisdom and navigation skills were as essential as tennis playing, teaching, business, and industry knowledge. I was 23 years old and PTR's first Director of Development actively traveling North America leading 2-day certification workshops while managing field staff and other organization projects. At a young age, I was exposed to real-life situations tennis professionals were experiencing that were scary and often career-altering.

At an age when I thought I knew it ALL (after all I had taught 5 summers, already worked as a private club head pro, Division 1 college coach, achieved a collegiate national ranking etc.), these real-world scenarios showed me that I "did not know what I did not know" in developing a healthy tennis career with longevity and professional success. The advantage of seeing firsthand career situations of notable multigenerational tennis professionals unfold before me provided essential tennis career skills that later contributed to my own success.

The truth is that even the best tennis professionals eventually experience career-changing events that are difficult to avoid. When tennis industry statics reveal that the average tennis job duration is 3-4 years it becomes only a matter of time and circumstances that career-minded tennis professionals need help.

I first met Coach Jack Thompson in the early 90's at the PTR International Tennis Symposium & $25,000 Championships on Hilton Head Island at the Van der Meer tennis center. In addition to being an accomplished clay-court player, I remember his dedication and joy of learning while effortlessly sharing information about our profession, teaching and coaching a variety of teaching pros.

Later in my career as a country club tennis director, women's pro tournament owner & USTA mid-Atlantic president, Jack Thompson was well known as an expert in our profession where coaches and players referenced him from on-court interactions over a dozen years prior in Staunton, VA as well as his current work in Charlotte, NC and Mooresville, NC. Such leadership and noted expertise are some of the reasons that in 2001 Jack received the exclusive lifetime recognition award of PTR International Master Professional.

Jack joined my own network of invaluable experts that I personally relied on to help me navigate situations and developments in my career. Jack always had time for my calls and communications in his genuine effort to help. Later as chair of PTR's International Master

Professional committee, I valued Jack's ability to objectively and professionally evaluate member candidates in his role on the selection committee and on our faculty team, conducting mentoring events on-site with international attendees.

Jack's book is a valuable "reference book" for all in our profession! Its chapters provide sage advice and "gold nuggets" of wisdom that readers receive to help them avoid such lessons the hard way via work-altering & costly situations. Not only do I recommend that all tennis professionals have a copy of this book, but I also strongly suggest they utilize it to create their own career guide. It can be reviewed during each year's seasons while adding additional career advice and industry knowledge in its supplemental pages to create their own custom career guide.

This book immediately will benefit the reader in their professional endeavors. Those in pursuit of a successful career in tennis should study many chapters of this book, especially those relating to:

- Creating your own mentorship advisory group to help you navigate your specific career minefields as they appear & unfold.

- Establishing & cultivating a professional niche that directly connects to your passion & joy vs. what's momentarily popular or seemingly earns more money.

- The importance of confidently bringing all ages of new players into the game who have not played before (vs. only being able to work with those who are already tennis players) – a challenge for many pros!

- Establishing lifelong learning habits to continually grow professionally and demonstrate expert communication skills on-court and from active listening.

- Living within your financial means and the cultural strata of your client environment where you are able to regularly grow savings that provide career choices, flexibility and valuable time-off for professional health.

The rewards of a successful tennis career are many! Jack Thompson deserves our thanks for writing this book so we may all have more ability to avoid career-altering minefields and to navigate job-threatening situations that escalate (and they will for all of us). His advice of creating your own advisory group will bring calm & confidence in many career areas given our professions unlimited areas of expected knowledge mastery.

Enjoy your journey and congratulations for demonstrating career wisdom by reading these pages and investing towards 'Building a Successful Tennis Career'.

John Raker, PTR International Master Professional
30-year tennis business owner & tennis industry educator
Country Club, municipal program, D1 college coach & pro tournament director
20+ years USTA national committee member & 2-term USTA MAS President
Former PTR Vice President, North America

Table of Contents:

Appendices:

Appendix I: Overly Involved Tennis Parents - More Common Today Than in the Past

Appendix II: 10 Most Common Mistakes Made by Tennis Professionals

Appendix III: Are American Coaches Using Too Many Dead Ball Drills?

Appendix IV: A Better Model for Developing Female Tennis Players

Appendix V: Preventing Tennis Elbow

Appendix VI: Sample Assistant Pro's Resume

Appendix VII: We Still Need to Fix American Tennis

Building a Successful Tennis Career:

A practical guide on surviving and prospering as a teaching professional

Introduction

This is not a book about how to teach tennis strokes or strategy. It is not about equipment or how to improve a player's fitness or mental toughness. While these subjects are occasionally broached, they are explored only in general terms. There are many fine books and resources on these topics, some of which I endorse in Chapter 16.

This book is, as the title suggests, about how you can have a successful career as a tennis teaching professional. It covers topics you're never taught in college and will not learn from the certification process, a specialty course or internship. It is a pragmatic guide on how to avoid the mistakes made by many well-intentioned tennis pros who have lost jobs. It is also a blueprint for the kind of things pros **should** do. These include tips regarding teaching, marketing, communication, human relations, designing and implementing programs and supervising staff. It is about how to ensure your long-term success in this field.

One can learn more if this book is read from front to back. The recommendations in this text are the culmination of my 40 years (and counting) experience in the tennis industry. As you will note, many ideas/suggestions come from my colleagues. Some of these pros have had careers of 15-30 years continuous employment at one club!

The average tenure of a tennis professional is now 3 to 4 years at any given club. Teaching, coaching, and managing programs present many challenges that didn't exist 20 years ago. Knowing how to successfully deal with these situations can ensure your survival. Indeed, if you can handle these "opportunities" appropriately, you'll actually prosper in today's tennis marketplace!

Chapter I

"Whether you fall in the extrovert or introvert category (or somewhere in between) — It can have a significant influence on your career choice, relationships and overall lifestyle."

Psychology Today

"Knowing yourself is the beginning of all wisdom."

Aristotle

Chapter I: Psychological Considerations in Teaching Tennis

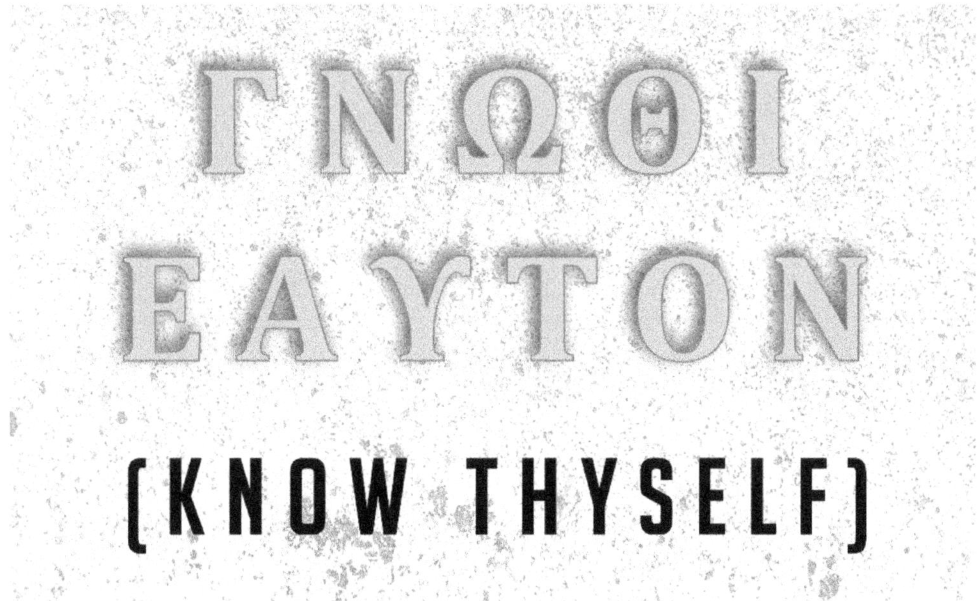

The overwhelming majority of tennis teaching positions involve long periods of social interaction. As you will learn in later chapters, how effectively you can meet this challenge could determine your success and longevity in the tennis industry.

If you are interested in a Director's or Head Pro's position, you need to ask yourself these questions: "Will I be able to endure the daily grind of socially interacting with my clientele?" "Will I be able to make speeches?" (e.g., at banquets, award assemblies, club parties and events). "If I'm sitting at a table and someone asks me a question like: "tell us about the weirdest thing that ever happened to you on a tennis court", — will I be comfortable to elaborate?". Such situations can be very stressful if you're an introvert, as suddenly everyone at the table is staring at you!

There's no getting around it: a tennis professional's job is a VERY social position, so if you can't answer the above questions in the affirmative, either look for another job or consider an Assistant's job, preferably one that involves teaching mainly privates or very small groups.

Incidentally, if you are an introvert, it doesn't necessarily mean that you can't succeed as a Director of Tennis or Head Pro. Some of the best pro's I have known have been introverts. These are just questions you need to address before entering the tennis profession.

Still interested in teaching tennis? Then read on!

Chapter 2

"The two most important days in your life are the day you were born and the day you figure out why."

Mark Twain

"You cannot control your level of talent, but you can control the amount of work you invest in reaching your goals. Working harder and longer will give you a tremendous competitive advantage. Because most people are unwilling to do this, your willingness to exert extraordinary effort can be your surest means to success."

Dr. Allen Fox

Chapter 2: So, You Want to be a Tennis Professional?

"The most important ingredient for success in the tennis profession, or any profession for that matter is having a passion for what you're doing."

Nick Saviano
PTR International Master Professional; excerpt from acceptance speech for "Touring Coach of the year" 2015 PTR International Tennis Symposium.

This quote says it all. It doesn't really matter what profession you choose – if you don't have a passion for what you're doing, you'll never achieve lasting success. In fact, it's highly unlikely you'll be able to attain short term success. Passion for improving your client's play is what it's all about. It's not about YOU – or how good a player you are. It's the passion you exude for helping your students improve their strokes, their knowledge of strategy and tactics, and the confidence and self-esteem they gain from learning a sport they can enjoy all their lives. It's also about teaching character, self-reliance, independence, integrity, honesty and how to recover from failure. It's about embracing the challenge of designing and implementing programs and activities that your clientele will enjoy. It also involves your serving as a good role model for your club and community.

If this describes you, then you're a good candidate for this profession. If you think that you'll be getting a job that's easy, that you'll be playing tennis whenever you'd like, that you'll be working 40 hours per week, and teaching all the best players, and that there will be little or no stress – then read no further. You need to choose another profession.

While there are many aspects of being a tennis professional that are immensely rewarding, there are also many things that make it exceedingly difficult. As one of my good friends (and a former country club president) Frank Eason, once said to me, "I don't know how you tennis pro's do it – the women expect you to look like Brad Pitt, all the members expect you to be able to play like John McEnroe and be able to teach them and their children to play like pros with little or no practice on their part!" This statement has an element of truth – at many clubs (particularly county clubs) today, you're only as good as your last great clinic/event. That's why it's so important that your education prepares you for a career as a tennis professional.

Chapter 3

"The future depends on what you do today."

Mahatma Gandhi

"If one's reputation is a possession, then of all my possessions, my reputation means the most to me."

Arthur Ashe

Chapter 3: Getting Started

If you are a senior in high school or freshman in college and you've made the decision to become a tennis professional, here are my suggestions regarding college:

1) Select an undergraduate major within the discipline of Physical Education, such as Sport Management, Exercise and Sports Science, Recreation with a minor in Teaching/Education. If I had to recommend one over the others, it would be Physical Education (the broad major) or Exercise and Sports Science. My rationale for this? Good teaching is both an art and a science. Course work in these areas will aid your understanding of the science of teaching tennis and all motor skills. The "art" of teaching comes from your creativity and experience.

2) There are currently 10 colleges in the United States that offer a Professional Tennis Management major. These include: Hope College, Methodist University, Berry College, Bridgewater State University, Ferris State University, Manhattanville College, University of Central Florida, San Diego State University, University of Florida and Queens College, City University.

3) Mentorship Opportunities: Find the best coaches/teachers in your area and learn from

them. Offer to help them with a study/class/clinic. Try to get an internship with them (paid or unpaid). If the college tennis coach has an excellent reputation, you may be able to assist him/her. I was lucky – when I attended college (Virginia Tech 1971-1977), I was able to work under Dr. Don Sebolt, as both an undergraduate and graduate student. Dr. Sebolt was the men's tennis coach from 1965-1971, and he was a superb teacher of all sports skills. Additionally, he was on the cutting edge of tennis research at the time. My apprenticeship – aiding him with his research and watching him teach – greatly influenced my career. I copied certain elements of his (and later Dennis Van Der Meer's and Pete Collins') teaching and over the years, adding my own personal touches in developing my own teaching style.

If you have already graduated from college and don't have this preparation, there are opportunities to strengthen your background. For instance, the **International Tennis Performance Association (ITPA) certification** is excellent. Your study for the appropriate level of certification will substantially enhance your development as a teacher. **The USTA's High Performance Tennis Coaching** certification is another option. **CSCS**, (Certified Strength and Conditioning Specialist) is also good, however a thorough undergraduate and graduate background in Physical Education is strongly advised before attempting this certification.

Tennis Teaching Certification: PTR **or USPTA**

Teaching certification in the tennis profession is an absolute must. No respectable business will hire you without it. You have 3 viable options: The Professional Tennis Registry (PTR); the United States Professional Tennis Association (USPTA), or both (dual certification).

Both are great organizations, but there are differences between the two. PTR is a global (and, at present, the largest) organization with more than 15,600 certified teaching professionals in 126 countries. The overwhelming membership in the USPTA is in the United States. PTR presently offers 5 education and certification pathways (10 and under, 11 to 17, Adult Development, Performance and Senior Development) – The USPTA has just one for teaching pros. It offers certification for other types of coaches (e.g., platform teams, recreational coaches, etc.) The PTR has a "Master of Tennis" level of achievement (sort of like a master's degree) within each certification pathway – the USPTA does not. Each organization also has a Master Professional (PTRs are "International Master Professional") rating. This is the highest level of achievement/certification attainable within these organizations. In fact, there are only 33 of us who have achieved PTR International Master Professional status as of this writing. The USPTA has 75 Master Professionals. In pointing out these differences, I'm simply providing factual information to aid the reader in making informed choices.

The PTR offers certification workshops in each state – the entire process takes 2 days and culminates with the certification exam. Membership in both organizations provides you with liability insurance which is extremely important in today's tennis industry. For specific information on testing/certification, visit www.PTRtennis.org and/or www.USPTA.com.

If you fail to achieve the highest level of certification the first time, you can retake the exam (the subpar parts) and seek to upgrade at a future point. Doing so within a year or two is what I advise – this keeps you trying to improve. and the test will be fresh in your mind. The longer you wait, the harder it is to get motivated to re-test.

It's extremely important to understand that certification is the *beginning* of your career. Continually educating yourself is a must! Becoming a great tennis professional should be thought of as a journey – not a destination! In my opinion, far too many pros stop trying to improve after becoming certified. Apparently, they feel as if they've 'arrived'. They fail to attend any professional/developmental conferences and never seek to further their education. This is a huge mistake – and it's particularly true of young pros today. Whether you're young or old, you should pursue every opportunity to expand your knowledge. Following this advice will put you ahead of your peers and it's the best means to ensure professional success, stability, and contentment. Perhaps Coach John Wooden put it best. He said, "When I am through learning, I am through."

You'll need a well-constructed resume in order to be considered for employment. I have included a sample Assistant Pro's 'resume' in Appendix VI.

A 'resume' is a record of your tennis experience (education, playing, teaching and other tennis related activities.) Be sure to list *all* your tennis accomplishments and provide (in the reference section) all names of those who can verify your experience and speak knowledgeably about your character and work ethic.

Finding Employment Opportunities

If you are a member of the PTR or USPTA, you have access to their job listings. Other methods of search include 1) friends or other tennis professionals, 2) ProTennisJobs.com, 3) college coaches, 4) members of clubs who are aware of a vacancy at their club or other clubs, 5) parents of junior players, 6) club management companies, 7) the USTA, 8) the NCAA job listings site, 9) directors/owners of junior tennis academies and 10) city parks and recreation departments.

Interviewing

There have been countless books, articles, and videos on the subject of how to interview, so in this section I present some subtle (and some not so subtle) considerations when interviewing.

1) <u>Do not drive a 'junker' to the interview.</u> Conversely, don't drive a BMW, Mercedes, or Jaguar etc. A dent free, 'middle of the road' sedan is best. Members at a club (particularly a country club) don't want you to exude wealth or celebrity status – nor do they want you to look poor. Rent a car if you have to.

2) <u>Dress to impress.</u> Do not wear clothing that looks dated or has stains (the 'stay dri' weaves used in tennis clothing today – especially the whites – hold stains permanently). Dress conservatively, and if possible, carry your tennis clothing with you. Arrive early. Be sure to wear new or near new shoes. Be prepared to change into tennis clothing in case the director wants to see how you hit. If you have a tennis bag, make sure it is clean as well. Also, many tennis players have an extremely strong grip and candidates should be cautious of squeezing too hard.

3) <u>During the interview, look the person/people you are addressing directly in the eyes.</u> Doing so conveys honesty and confidence. Do not – at any time – stare at the floor. Interview skills take practice – you may want to practice with someone prior to the interview.

4) <u>Do not cross your arms.</u> It is fine to express yourself with hand movements as long as they're not excessive.

5) <u>Convey that you are intensely interested in people/customer satisfaction.</u> Throughout the interview express that you love to teach and see people improve. Stress that you enjoy the challenge of building and maintaining tennis programs – that it doesn't matter who you teach – young, middle aged, old – beginner to high level players. In discussing the junior program, let the interviewers know that you consider teaching character, honesty, integrity, self-reliance, independence and how to recover from failure to be just as important as teaching strokes and strategy.

6) <u>Have a list of questions to ask.</u> Examples include: How many members? Average age of the members? How many juniors and adults, etc.

7) <u>Know who you are and act accordingly.</u> The southern states, northern states, mid-west and far west states have unique social mores and customs. Act in accordance with the area in which you're interviewing. For instance, in the south where I was born, raised and reside, it is commonplace to say, 'yes ma'am, no sir', etc. when answering anyone older than you. Also, when disagreeing with someone, Southerners are generally a bit more polite (e.g., "I respectfully disagree"). In the North, life is more hurried and as a

rule, people are more blunt. It's perfectly fine to respond to someone – young or old up North with a simple yes or no. If you disagree when debating an issue in the North, it's fine to say, "I disagree with you!" In summary: "when in Rome, do as the Romans do."

8) <u>At the end of the interview, thank the interviewer(s) for their time.</u>

Accepting a Position

There are needs that must be met in order for you to be happy and successful in a job.

These include:

1) Acceptance: You need to feel you'd be accepted as a person and professional – that you'll "fit in" at the club.

2) Importance: You have to feel that the job is an important one – that the club views the program as essential.

3) Security: You have to feel that your compensation is fair/reasonable and that there is the opportunity for advancement or stability in the position for a job well done.

Think of your ability to perform as a three-legged stool with each leg representing one of the above needs. If any one leg is removed, the stool fails – and you will too.

To illustrate, let me share a story.

A few years ago, a friend of mine (a highly accomplished pro with more than 30 years' experience in all facets of club tennis and an outstanding coaching record with all types of players) accepted a job at a fairly high-profile club. The tennis committee had recently hired a management company to oversee club operations. My friend was hired by the management company.

It was immediately apparent that the situation was very disorganized. No one had a job description and there wasn't even a recognized (written) organizational structure. My friend – who had the experience – offered to write up job descriptions and an organizational flow chart. The management company director gave him the go ahead, and after reviewing it, approved the completed work. My friend's job description had him reporting to the newly appointed director of tennis, who was roughly 28, and whose only experience was the 3 years he had spent as an assistant pro at the club.   He, in turn, reported to the director.   The pro shop/membership/marketing director (who happened to be the wife of the management company director) reported to her husband.

My friend didn't have a good feeling from the start. Immediately after turning in the job descriptions, he started getting directives from the wife, the director of tennis and the director of the management company (the dilemma of having multiple bosses is discussed in detail in a later chapter).   The orders were often conflicting. In a short period of time, my friend began feeling insecure. His concern was heightened when his first several paychecks arrived late.

He was assigned 5 group lesson – predominately with older ladies and given no directions whatsoever on what type of clinic(s) the various groups liked/expected. So, he did the only thing he or anyone else could have done – ask the group for a consensus on what they wanted: instructional, drilling, playing, etc. All the groups went well except one. A woman in one of the groups, who had voted for an instructional lesson became problematic. She went to the next tennis committee meeting (keep in mind, my friend had only been on the job 3 ½ weeks) and complained that he had talked too much (in an instructional lesson??!) during the clinic.

Five days later, my friend was called in by the director of the management company and told that he would be 'reassigned' to other duties within their organization. This change translated to a $12,000 cut in pay. In short order, my friend turned in his 2-week notice. He immediately found a better job, closer to home – and he's been happy and in the job for 4 years now.

What can you learn from this? If you are the potential employee – **be sure to do your homework!** If you feel the job isn't right – if it's unprofessional, - if the person you'd be reporting to is "learning the ropes" as s/he goes along, if there's a questionable track record at the club, if they've had trouble keeping employees, if they have a bad reputation within the community of tennis professionals or if they've had a record of paying people late – then don't accept the job!

If you're a director or administrator – what can be learned from this example? This is perhaps the quintessential bad management story! The management company director didn't follow the organizational structure that **he** had approved! The message that one person (out of 5 groups) was upset should have been communicated to my friend by his immediate superior – the young director of tennis.   Feedback was not given to my friend in a timely manner – 5 days is too long! The tennis committee should have told the disgruntled player to speak to the director of tennis. The director of the management company (who was present at the tennis committee meeting) should have told the woman: "let me check with the director of tennis and he will get back with you."

As an administrator, you give an employee every reasonable chance to fix what's wrong. Barring a catastrophic incident (e.g., an affair with a club member, accusation of sexual harassment, stealing, gross insubordination) it usually takes an employee one year to settle into a new job.

Incidentally, since my friend left the club five years ago, they have been through six different head pros (they're now on their 7th!) That's an average of a new head pro every 7 months. The club's programs have suffered, and at a time where the other area clubs have flourished. Clearly, there are management problems! Unfortunately, stories such as this are much more common than you might think.

In summary, to do well in a job, you must feel accepted, important, and secure. If you don't, keep your present job until you can find another one that meets these needs.

Your First Job

In all likelihood, you'll need to start in an entry level position. I was extremely fortunate – my first tennis job was a director's position. This was both a good and bad situation – good because it forced me to learn quickly (much through trial and error) how to budget, manage people, deal with an owner and the public etc. It was bad, because I could have profited from being an understudy to an experienced director and thereby could have avoided many of the mistakes that I made early in my career.

If your first job is entry level, expect your hours to be long, expect there to be manual labor duties and plan on teaching a lot of lower skilled students. That's just the way it is. Do not expect to land the big paying, prestigious job right away. You'll have to pay your dues and establish a good track record at your first job (and in some cases your second and third jobs) before you can move up. Have patience. Do the best you can at each position, and you'll be rewarded with better paying jobs.

Stay within the parameters of the duties in <u>your</u> job description. Be concerned with doing the best possible job that YOU can do. Don't worry about how others are doing at their jobs – that's not your business! The working world would be so much better if everyone would just follow this simple rule. There is an exception to this; if someone's poor job performance compromises your ability to do a good job (ex. – clay court maintenance staff isn't doing good work – and your customers are complaining), then you should report it to the appropriate supervisor.

Assistant Pro: Be a Good Team Player!

As previously mentioned, your first tennis job will likely be as an assistant pro. In this, as in any position, it is crucial to be a good team player. You are there to carry out the directives of the head pro/director of tennis in the manner in which s/he prescribes. It **is not** your job to change their plans unless they solicit your input. You should be loyal and realize that the director/head Pro's success is essential to your success. In other words, you should be a good team player! At all costs, avoid assigning blame when something goes wrong. If responding to a client or member's complaint which is the director's or head pro's fault, simply state, "we'll find out what went wrong and make it right for you."

I have seen cases where assistant pros have tried (and a few succeeded in the short term) to get their supervisors fired in the hope they'd be promoted. This shows extremely poor character, a lack of integrity and it rarely works. In the long run, it hurts the assistant's career – s/he is quickly labeled untrustworthy and may end up with no career in tennis at all. **Good tennis programs emanate from a cohesive teaching staff that has good communication skills and respect for one another.** A note to head pros and directors of tennis: If you discover that your assistant is insubordinate, fire him/her immediately! Do not try to 'fix them'. They can't be fixed. The personality traits that underlie their insubordinate actions (selfishness, self-centeredness, lack of integrity, dishonesty, and lack of empathy) were developed around age 3-5 and nothing you can do or say is going to change that. Given a second chance, they'll do it again!

Early in my career as a director, I had an employee who was grossly insubordinate. Indeed, she attempted a coup in the hopes of getting my job. Without going into all the details, suffice it to say, it failed miserably. Her actions alienated her from her fellow employees and most wanted to see her go. I handled the situation by talking it over with the owner of the club (my direct supervisor) and his opinion was to fire her. I told him I wanted to give her another chance to which he replied "Jack – you can do what you want – but my experience in these matters is: a tiger never changes its stripes!" As it turned out, he was right. She ended up having problems with other employees (in one case, she got into a brawl with a woman on the janitorial staff) and quit within 6 months.

The moral of the story should be apparent: **Do not hold onto disloyal/ insubordinate/dishonest employees!** Let them go! – Keeping them only prolongs the inevitable and makes you appear as a weak leader.

Tips on Hiring

It can be hard to hire good help, and for any given position there's usually no shortage of applicants. Why is it so hard to hire? In my opinion, and that of many of my colleagues, many young people today lack a good work ethic and have a sense of entitlement. It's fairly common for an assistant pro – even a recent hire – to tell you, "I can't help with this weekend's clinic because I am going to (for example) the beach." They don't ask their supervisors – they tell them! This is the type of person you should avoid hiring.

Illustrative of this are the experiences of my colleague, Mark Allen, who is a seasoned tennis professional. Mark graduated from UNCC and played 2 years on the Men's Tennis Team.

Upon graduating, he entered the corporate world (sales and marketing) and retired early to pursue a career in tennis. By any standard, he has been highly successful. Six years ago, he took over a fledgling tennis program at the Sportscenter in Concord, NC and has increased participation over 300%! Additionally, he now manages three other clubs/programs and owns/operates profitable pro shops at each site. I asked Mark his views on hiring tennis staff to which he responded, "I look for four things when I hire."

1) **Can the prospective employee do the job?** Does s/he have the knowledge and experience to do a good job?

2) **Will they do the job?** Does s/he have the work ethic – the stick-to-it-ness to make our program successful? At this point, you must share the written job description with them. You have to ensure s/he has a complete understanding of all the job duties required of the position.

3) **Will the person be a good team fit?** Is s/he customer driven? Will s/he be able to get along with the staff?

4) Finally, **will the candidate be willing to pursue continuing education?** When asked why it's so hard to hire good people, Mark responded: "I think that people today – particularly those aged 40 and younger are technology driven/competent. My generation and older are relationship driven. We were taught by our parents and teachers how to interact with people and that good communication skills were crucial to success. We were also taught that doing for others before self was of paramount importance. Regrettably, I think these skills are not being embraced by young people, because they're not being taught. Consequently, we're seeing a generation of kids who are somewhat self-centered, want immediate success, with a mediocre to poor work ethic. There **are** good young employees out there – they're just hard to find. You've really got to do your homework, check people's backgrounds, etc., when hiring today!"

If you're hiring a young person, it should be obvious what can be gained from Mark's advice. More importantly, to get a job, you must – above all – convince the person/people hiring that you'll do whatever it takes to get the job done, that you have good human relations skills, and that you're a good team player.

Reducing the Likelihood of a Bad Hire

No matter how much experience you have in hiring, you'll never reach the point where you're 100% successful in hiring people. You can, however, significantly reduce the chances of employing the wrong people by:

1) **Checking references**. This, however, is just a starting point. Former employers are

reluctant today to give bad references for fear of legal retribution. My advice is to always ask the question, "Knowing what you know now, would you hire this person?"

2) **Beware of charlatans**. As long as there have been teachers of tennis, there have been those who fabricate or embellish their accomplishments. Unfortunately, it's become much more common in the past 2 decades and this is confirmed by many of my colleagues. It's all too common today to hear of cases where a pro/coach or "consultant" claims to be PTR, USPTA, CSCS, ACSM, or ITPA certified and is not. This is odd – especially when you consider how easy it is to verify the accuracy of someone's background via the internet or phone call (s).

Recently, I had such a situation happen to me. About 3 years ago, I had the opportunity to work with someone claiming to have an extensive educational background in exercise physiology. This person also claimed to be CSCS (certified strength and conditioning specialist) and ACSM (American College of Sports Medicine) certified. Furthermore, they said they had served as a fitness consultant to one of the top collegiate tennis teams in the country.

A simple check revealed the following:

- The college this person attended never has offered a major (undergraduate or graduate) in exercise physiology. They don't even offer a major in physical education.

- This person did not hold certification as CSCS or ACSM.

- Most disturbing of all, the college where this person claimed to be a "strength training consultant" was a complete lie! A call to the coach (who I knew) revealed that they were at the school only one day – looking for work. I also spoke to the head strength coach, and he stated that this person had never helped the tennis coach or their staff in any way! Indeed, he said "I don't know such a person."

Without going into further detail, suffice it to say that 90% of this person's resume was falsified. Needless to say, I declined the offer to work with him. My advice to you is: Always check out – thoroughly – a person's background! As the old saying goes – "you can expect what you inspect."

3) **Checking with former members** of the club(s) where the candidate was employed.

4) **Asking area pros their thoughts** on the candidate's qualifications and interpersonal skills

5) **Having at least one face to face interview** – ask pointed questions about their work ethic, customer relations and teaching philosophy.

Every time you decide to hire a person, make sure you have a very complete job description for them. The last sentence under "Job Responsibilities/Specific Duties" should read: Other duties as defined by the director/head pro (whichever the case may be) as needed.

Getting back to the three needs identified earlier- (acceptance, importance, and security) – it's vitally important early in a new hire's employment that you compliment them on something that they do well. By doing so, you give them a sense of being important and foster self-confidence.

Finally, remember that no matter how cautious you are in your background check, etc., sometimes the person just doesn't work out. Hiring an employee is a little like receiving a birthday gift. The size of the box, print on the wrapping paper and bow can all look great, but once you open the box, it might not be something you want. Be sure to give your new hire a fair chance before making the decision to let them go. As previously stated, barring anything catastrophic, it may take as long as 12 months for an employee to fully adjust to a new job. Along the way, however, make sure to document all instances of an employee's failure to carry out their job duties and indicate what actions you took as a consequence.

Letting Someone Go

Firing someone is a terrible experience. If you're normal, your emotions will run the gamut – everything from sorrow, guilt, and dread, to fear and procrastination.

The first time I had to let someone go, I was 27 and had been a manager for roughly three years. I couldn't sleep the night before and was a nervous wreck leading up to the termination meeting. As it turned out, the employee knew it was coming and had already secured other employment which made the whole situation much easier. Nevertheless, it will cause you stress. If it doesn't, perhaps you're not a good fit for a management position. Why do I feel this way? In order to succeed in this business, you have to care about people! With each firing, it may become easier – but it's never comfortable.

If you find yourself having to terminate someone, the following advice from my friend Jon Post, should help. Jon owned and operated a very successful on-line pharmacy business for many years. He said, "If you must fire someone, I've found it's best to get right to the point. The first 4 to 5 people I had to let go, I'd try to 'ease' into the topic, but when I did this, people would realize they were being fired, and they'd be even more stressed out…so what's the point in taking this approach? Prolonging the inevitable is senseless – just get to the point: 'Mary… I think you're a wonderful person, - but as you know, things haven't been working out. I'm going to have to let you go.' Do let the employee know (if they're deserving of a good recommendation), that you'd be happy to serve as a reference. Likewise, if you're unwilling to serve a reference, say so up front.

When you're considering terminating someone, be sure to document each instance where the employee failed to perform their duties – include the date, day and time of the infraction and the action you took. Give the employee every opportunity to improve – sometimes people get markedly better after a rocky start. Some shortcomings however, mandate immediate dismissal (e.g., an affair with a married club member, gross insubordination, embezzlement, fighting, sexual harassment, etc.).

On a separate note, if an employee leaves on their own and they've been a good employee, ask the question "From your experience what can we do or cease doing to improve our tennis program?" Their response doesn't necessarily warrant change – it's just for consideration.

Chapter 4

"Making money is a happiness. And that's a great incentive. Making other people happy is a super-happiness."

Muhammad Yunus

"Success is getting what you want, while happiness is wanting what you get."

Author unknown

Chapter 4: Sources of Revenue for the Tennis Professional

There are a number of revenue streams available to tennis professionals. The following is a partial list in order from the most to the least profitable. Without a doubt, you'll come up with other ways of increasing your earnings. The only thing that'll limit you will be the extent of your imagination.

1) **Lessons /Clinics/Camps:** This is the best source of income. Your only cost (s) will be balls and (if a large group is being taught), the fee necessary for additional help. **Have good balls in all the hoppers. Dead balls make you look cheap and less professional.**

   a) The Tennis Court and Safety Concerns. Like a public-school teacher, you are responsible for the safety of your students. As you enter the court area to teach a lesson or clinic try to spot things that could potentially cause an accident. Examples include broken fencing, net post crank handles (if possible, should be adjusted parallel to the net post, removed or a ball placed over the crank handle); ball can lids, insect/bees' nests in posts/fencing (particularly prevalent in the summertime), broken glass, etc.). Fix these situations immediately!

2) **Stringing:** Invest in a good, spring-loaded floor model stringing machine. In my view, the pneumatic machines are not worth it due to their high cost. You'll have to stock string, but you'll turn it over quickly. Join the USRSA. It's worth it, membership gives you access to their stringing book (tells you how to string any racquet) and access to their

knowledgeable staff. Depending on where you live, you can make $15-$25/racquet. Once proficient, you'll be able to string a racquet in about 30 minutes.

3) **Consulting** - for other clubs or individuals can be very profitable. I've been a consultant since 1988, and during that time I have had about 20 jobs. Your expertise can be used in any number of areas: facility feasibility, facility design, operations efficiency, program design and hiring qualified staff. Be sure that your general manager, director, and board is ok with your doing consulting work. What you charge should be a function of what the market will bear and will be on a project or job basis. I would strongly suggest developing a website for your consulting business. It should be common sense that you don't consult with any clubs that are in direct competition with your place of employment.

4) **Pro Shop**: Approximately 80% of all tennis pro shops are partially or completely owned by clubs – and there's a good reason for it. Pro shops (particularly those with a sizeable inventory of clothing, shoes, and racquets) are a losing proposition. I've known **lots** of pros who have lost out on pro shops! TRUST ME, do not stock shoes or clothing. As far as racquets, just carry demos. Your clientele can order when s/he determines what's a good fit. If management is adamant about stocking clothing, shoes, and racquets, propose the following:

   a) The club owns the hard goods (clothing, racquets, shoes). They give you a budget – you stock accordingly. The club keeps 75-80% of the profit from the sales and you keep 20-25%. If there's a loss, you don't get any compensation for the time spent with the hard goods, but you don't have to pay the club anything either.

   b) You own/stock the accessories (socks, wrist bands, head bands, grips, head tape, vibration dampeners, etc.). You keep 100% of the revenue associated with these sales and all revenue from racquet stringing.

5) **Special clinics conducted at other clubs:** For this you'll have to have exceptional expertise (and be recognized by your peers as an expert) in a specialty area in tennis. For instance, Pete Collins is an acknowledged expert in teaching doubles. He has been able to travel the world teaching his "Successful Doubles" and "Advanced Successful Doubles" courses. I have been able to do the same, offering clinics within my area of expertise, tennis specific strength training and conditioning. Again, be sure you have the GM/board approval for clinics conducted at other clubs.

6) **Books:** You won't get rich writing tennis books, but it can be very rewarding, can strengthen your 'resume' and can provide some additional revenue, particularly if the book fills a niche that others have not.

In summary, most of your income will (and should) come from teaching. Avoid investing a lot in a pro shop. Most pros who do, find themselves spending long hours on the court to pay for inventory that just hangs on the racks.

Chapter 5

"You can't fit a round peg into a square hole."

Sydney Smith

"Plans are nothing, planning is everything."

Dwight D. Eisenhower

Chapter 5: Designing Effective Tennis Programs

Designing a tennis program must be specific to the needs of the club. For instance, the needs/interests of a country club where the mean age of the membership is 55 are very different from that of a public facility whose membership consists largely of young families. The specific activities of the program should reflect your clienteles' interest and needs.

If you are entering a job as an assistant professional, in all likelihood you'll probably be carrying out an already existing program. If, however, you're being employed as the head professional or director of tennis, you'll be expected to bring in innovative programs and activities. In such cases, the following things should be done:

1) Have a meeting with the tennis committee/manager/owner and invite a few influential players who represent the different playing interests at the club. Get their feedback as to what would make a better program. Do not use this as the sole determiner of the program's make-up, but rather one of such considerations.

2) Keep the programs/activities that have been successful/well attended.

3) Eliminate the programs/activities that have not been successful/well attended.

4) **Identify the needs of your clientele/membership**. If the overwhelming majority are 'hit and giggle' type players, then design the program to be more recreational in nature.

Have more socials and round robin activities. If the membership is more competitive, have more tournaments, leagues, ladders and USTA team play.

5) **Don't be reluctant to try new activities on an experimental basis**. As with any program, if it fails, eliminate or fine tune it and if it succeeds, keep it.

6) **Each year** have one or two guest pros – highly respected coaches or clinicians – come to your club to teach a clinic or two with you. The PTR has 33 International Master Pro's and the USTA has about 75 Master Professionals. This provides you with an unlimited resource base.   Call it the "Visiting Pro Clinic Series" or whatever title seems appropriate.   Offering this type of activity doesn't diminish your credibility as a teaching professional. To the contrary, it greatly enhances your stature.

A few ideas on Programmatic Activities

- Men's & Women's Drop-in Play Days

- Men's & Women's Quads

- Men's & Women's local "home and home" matches (your club plays a club at their site and later hosts that club at your site)

- Men's & Women's USTA League play

- Men's & Women's Team Clinic/practices

- Men's Night – a regular weekly drop-in play night. (Beer and jokes optional but highly recommended.)

- Cardio day/night class(es)

- Adult Tennis Camp(s)

- Adult "Tennis in a Weekend" Camp (for beginning adults or those looking to pick up the game after an extended layoff).

- Demo Days. Invite a sales rep to bring racquets the members can try out and order.

- As previously mentioned, Visiting Pro Clinics

- USTA sanctioned tournaments for adults and juniors.

- Universal Tennis Rating (UTR) tournaments

- Junior tennis camps

- High Performance Junior Tennis Academy/Camps

- Middle School and High School Tennis Coaches Clinics

- Weekend (Fri., Sat., or Sun.) Round Robins with a "theme" – example: "Battle of the Sexes."

- Woods and Whites Round Robin (where everyone must play with a wooden racquet)

- Member-Guest Tournament(s)

- Pro-Ams

- Pro Exhibitions

What You Should Not Offer

1) **Free programs.** It is my firm opinion that you should not offer any free programs and here's why:

   a) Only the miserly members will show up – the people who never take lessons. If you think that giving members a taste of what you can do will increase your lesson base – you're wrong! If the idea is that after a while, you'll start charging for a "free" program and get good attendance – you're wrong again. It'll wither and die.

   b) The majority attending the free program(s) will come to expect it – so if you try to end the program for any reason, they'll complain.

   c) Anything "free" is perceived as not being very good.

   It's better to charge for everything – your time and expertise are worth it! After all, do your members get ongoing free services from their doctor, dentist, lawyer or accountant? Of course not! Do not give away your greatest asset!

2) **Programs that fail to address the needs of your club members.** An example of this would be offering up a "Modern Tennis" clinic, teaching open stance Semi-Western to Full Western grips, heavy topspin, swinging volleys, etc. to a membership where the mean age is 55+. Likewise, teaching 3.0 level clinics to 4.0 – 4.5 players is a recipe for disaster. Know who your clientele are and teach/program to that level.

3) **Too much, too soon.** When starting at a new club, do **not** overload the membership with every idea you have in your head in one year! Start with a core of proven programs and gradually introduce a few new ideas with each passing year.

In summary, it is meeting the needs of the club membership that determines successful program design and implementation. Just because an activity was popular at a previous club doesn't mean that it'll work at your current one. Conversely, one that failed at your last club may prove to be a hit in your present situation.

Chapter 6

"Your career success in the workplace – independent of technical expertise – depends on the quality of your people skills."

Max Messmer, Jr.

"We are more advanced technologically than ever before. However, technology in many respects is leading to the decline of conversation."

Cindy Ann Peterson

Chapter 6: Customer Relations, Communicating with Members, Superiors, Peers, and Staff

A tennis professional's human relations skills are the bedrock of their success. Those who "have it" stay employed and those who don't will sooner or later have to change careers.

The best indicator of a pro's interpersonal skills is the length of time s/he is employed at a club. Many pros I know have logged 20 + years at their respective clubs.

One of these pros, Bill Francis, was kind enough to give me an interview regarding his thoughts on customer service. Bill is a highly successful Director of Tennis at the Country Club of Charlotte. He and his wife, Julie (who works in the pro shop and assists Bill) have been at CCC for 28 years.

I asked Bill the following questions:

Q. What factors do you attribute to your longevity at CCC?

A. I care deeply about our membership. I see them just like any other group of people – human beings with needs and emotions. It's our job to help them achieve their goals, whatever they may be. I've got a terrific staff now, perhaps the best ever! When we see a member coming

"

down the sidewalk to our pro shop, we don't just see dollar signs, we see a person that we truly enjoy interacting with and helping. We've been successful here, because we treat everyone the same, whether they take lessons or not. We treat the member who just plays or the member who just comes in on occasion to use the ball machine exactly the same as those who take a lot of lessons and buy merchandise from the pro shop. It's the little things, lots of little things that make up good human relation skills. Things like going out on a court and helping a member set up the ball machine, asking them about their family, sending them a handwritten note if they're injured. It's not always about making more money. Showing you care extends to filling in for a doubles group if you have the time to do so. I can't overemphasize how important it is to interact, through conversation (with the members), it's something that we work hard at doing every day!

Q. Having hired many assistant pros over the years, what reasons do you see when they fail?

A. I'd have to say that putting too much emphasis on the amount of money they make would be number one. Along with this would be a lack of time spent on the job. Most had the mentality that "I don't have a lesson, so I'm going home." The second reason most pros lose their job is an inability to relate to the members – not being able to or being unwilling to carry on conversations with them – not caring enough about the members and not treating all of them the same. Selfishness is another persistent problem I see – where pros put too much emphasis on their own game and not enough on their member's game. Finally, - there's the situation where the pro gets too close to certain members. This always backfires…essentially it boils down to them not treating all members the same!

Q. When you hire a new pro, is there anything in particular that you tell them?

A. At CCC, the employee receives a very thorough orientation through the human resources department. I do, however, make it a point of telling them that they must – above all- sincerely care about the members and that their actions must reflect this. I tell them that if they don't care, there's nothing I can do to save them (as employees).

Another career teaching professional with a long and successful employment history is Doug Eller of Hickory, NC. Doug's resume is an exemplary one: he began teaching tennis in 1977, and his employment timeline is decades at individual clubs. One day after we played tennis, Doug agreed to share his views on what it takes to be successful as a tennis pro:

Q. What do you see as the primary reasons some pros fail?

A. In many cases I see pros unwilling to adjust their teaching to the capabilities of the students with whom they work. A good example would be trying to teach a "Nadal" like forehand drive to a junior or adult who has mediocre to little athleticism. The student gets frustrated and so does the pro. Another reason why pros don't succeed is a failure to ask students what their goals are – and to structure their lessons accordingly. Perhaps the biggest reasons though are lack of good human relation skills and caring for the clients/members. To be successful, you must treat everyone the same – whether they take lessons or not. Staying organized, being on time and being honest are all virtues that lead to success.

Q. What advice would you have for a young person just learning the profession?

A. I would highly recommend that they find an internship/get a job as an assistant pro with a good, seasoned head pro, and that they learn the business!

I strongly agree with everything Bill and Doug say. I would, however, add one caveat: that you must **always** be alert to dissatisfied members/clients. Why? Studies show that a dissatisfied customer will tell an average of 7 to 10 other people about their negative experience. A satisfied customer tends to tell only 4 to 5 other acquaintances. As the old saying goes, "Bad news travels fast!" If you can fix the problem, though, the customer will usually tell 6 to 8 other people. Think about it! Most 'fixes' are simple, but if you reach an impasse with a customer, just ask them "What's going to make it right for you because if you're not happy, I'm not happy?" If the customer's request is reasonable (and it almost always will be), then grant it. In very rare instances, you may have an unreasonable request (I once had a member who wanted a year of free membership for a simple error in billing). In these cases, I recommend you say: "I'm not authorized to make that decision, let me run your idea by the GM and the board of directors. Doing this removes you from the line of fire.

To reiterate – do what's necessary to keep your customers happy, but once you learn about an upset customer – do everything you can (within policy) to rectify things.

Communicating with Superiors, Peers, and Staff

This is an extremely important aspect of any employment. Many tennis professionals have lost jobs because of an inability to get along with their coworkers and/or general manager. A tennis professional like any other employee must possess very good to excellent human relations skills. S/he must return messages in a timely manner, whether it comes from a superior, coworker, peer, or member. Most importantly, s/he should be concerned with doing the best job that s/he can do and not be concerned with assessing the job performance of others. No general manager likes it when a worker offers up their views on the work of employees in another department. That's the job of the GM!

I have seen many cases over the years where tennis pro's /directors of tennis have acted arrogantly. Through their actions and words, they come off as being indispensable or as having a job that's more difficult or more important than their peers. In every single case, these people were fired and most found it difficult to land another teaching job. Communicating with your superiors, subordinates, and peers in a professional manner, and in a way that reflects that you're part of the team, is absolutely crucial!

When it's time to move on (or knowing when to look for another position)

The days of a pro staying employed at one club for a lifetime are long gone. If you remain in the tennis profession, you'll probably change jobs 4-7 times during your career. Leaving a job will either occur on your terms or on your employer's terms.

If you accept a better job, be sure to tell your immediate supervisor first and give them **at least** two weeks' notice. If possible, four weeks' notice is preferred, and it goes a long way toward the manager giving you good future recommendations. Ask your manager how s/he wants to inform the membership of your leaving (i.e., you send an email, s/he sends an email, by word of mouth, via tennis committee, etc.), and tell no one until permission is given.

Being let go is a traumatic experience. If this happens, try to remain calm and act in a professional manner. Under no circumstances show anger or badmouth the club/owner/GM. This gets you nowhere. Just try to learn from the experience. Do not see yourself as a failure – if this were the case, then every collegiate or professional coach wouldn't get another job after being fired. People in every profession lose jobs every day – sometimes over very trivial matters. Liken your dismissal to losing a tennis match. After the loss, just get back up, dust yourself off and hop back in the saddle! History is replete with stories of coaches who lost jobs – sometimes multiple jobs – and went on to greatness!

If you are fired (and it's not offered) ask for some severance pay. Additionally, offer to stay for at least two weeks before leaving. However, in most cases, you'll be asked to leave immediately, or at the longest, within several days. It's tempting to leave your job immediately after the termination in retaliation, but do not do this. It's very unprofessional if management wants you to stay for a while – and it will be recorded in your employee file. As hard as it may be, thank the manager/owner for the time you had with them and say you're sorry it didn't work out. Following these suggestions makes it much easier to get another job.

Chapter 7

"True teachers are those who use themselves as bridges over which they invite their students to cross; then having facilitated their crossing, joyfully collapse, encouraging them to create their own."

Nikos Kazantzakis

"Practice doesn't make perfect – it only makes skills permanent. Only perfect practice makes perfect."

Vince Lombardi

Chapter 7: Teaching Concepts

There is a definite progression in developing a player's tennis game. I call it the developmental pyramid (see figure 1).

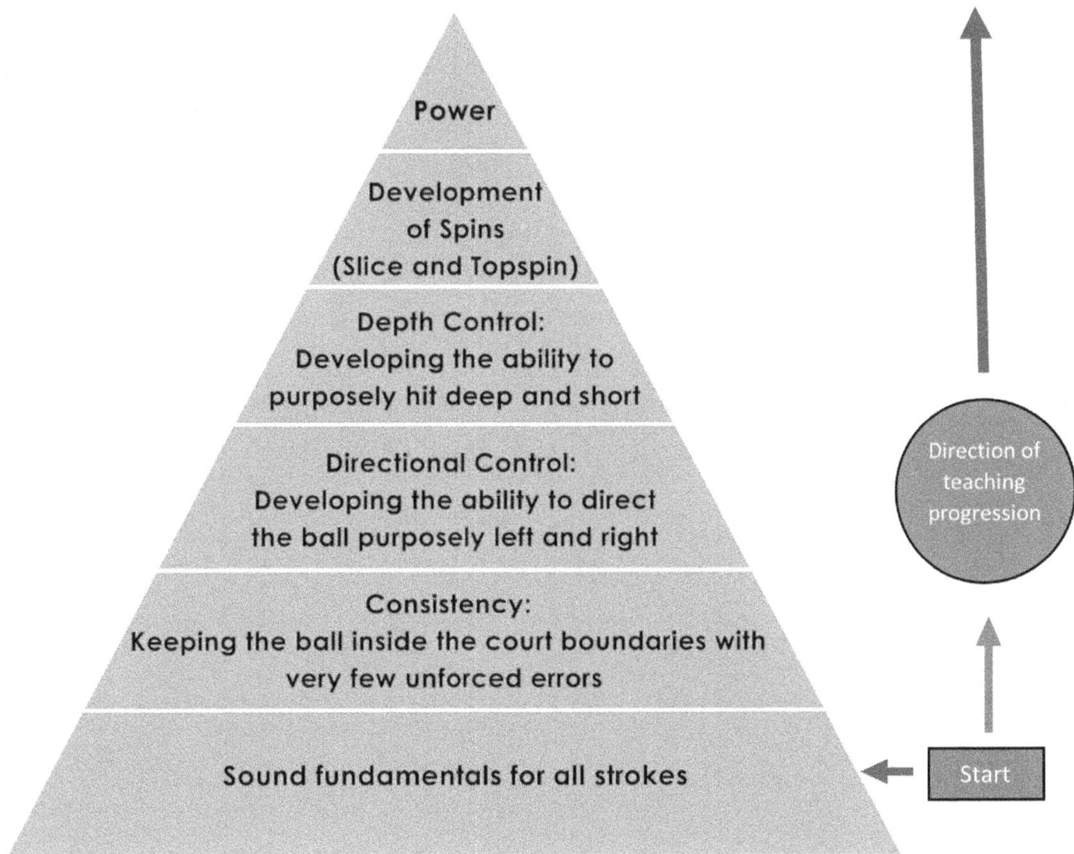

Figure 1: The Developmental Pyramid

Regardless of the type of student (adult, junior, male, or female), always start by teaching **sound fundamentals for all the primary strokes** (forehand drive, backhand drive, lob, serve, volley, overhead smash). This forms the base of the pyramid. These (primary) fundamentals include:

- acceptable grip for the stroke being taught.

- early shoulder turn (turning the shoulders is the <u>first physical action</u> that should occur for every stroke. For the serve, the shoulders already start sideways.

- sound footwork

- good balance

- consistent body spacing from the ball

- appropriate completion of backswing consistent with the style and type of stoke being taught

- consistent and correct point of contact for the stroke being learned

- vertical racquet face (i.e., perpendicular to the ground) at ball contact for drives

- following ball contact (on groundstrokes) – lengthy extension of the racquet face out to the target zone

- adequate trunk rotation for the stroke being learned

- good weight transfer at ball contact

- consistent point of follow through

In so far as teaching a particular 'style' of executing a stroke (especially the forehand drive), I advise the following:

- If the student is a senior player, or a junior with mediocre to poor athleticism – teach them the **simplest** way to hit consistently within the above listed fundamentals. Using the forehand drive as an example, - an Eastern forehand grip with a straight back to small loop backswing. Reserve semi-Western grips and semi-open to open stances for the better athletes, but even with these players, simplify the 'style' if you're getting bad results or feel that the stroke has no future.

- Trying to teach mediocre to poor athletes the "modern forehand" (a term that really is a misnomer – plenty of players during the 1920's hit like that) is a terrible mistake. It would be akin to trying to teach a poor athlete a reverse layup in basketball before learning the basic layup.

Getting back to the developmental pyramid – the next stage is to help the student develop **excellent consistency**. This means they must be able to sustain a rally of 15-20 shots (they hit 15-20 consecutively **somewhere** in the court.) *

Once this is attained, the pro should then teach his/her student(s) how to hit the ball purposefully cross-court or down-the-line **(directional control).**

The next stage is **depth control**. Students should now be taught how to purposely hit deep (I stress half-way between the service line and baseline as being good depth) and short (being able to hit a slow shot with underspin which bounces 2 times before crossing the service line).

The next objective – **learning spins** – can now be fully developed. Spins can be introduced earlier (even during the consistency phase), but only in rudimentary form. During this time, intensive work toward perfecting both slice and topspin on groundstrokes and slice and topspin for the service should be performed. Far too many pros devote almost no time to teaching slice. Consequently, what we are seeing today in the U.S. is a generation of juniors who lose matches due to their inability to slice well, return a slice that is well hit to them and who can't volley proficiently. **Spend time with your students building a complete game!** Doing so will make them far better players – they will have a means of changing strategy if what they're doing in a match is failing.

The final step in the developmental pyramid is teaching the student how and when to hit with **power**. I have seen many pros who attempt to get their students to swing hard from the beginning and this is an awful mistake. This can't work because it's in direct opposition to the scientific principles of motor learning. The "speed to error" ratio (among other principles) clearly states that **as swing speed increases errors increase**. That's the reason kids learn T-ball before attempting to play little league baseball. That's the reason a gymnast learning a new skill performs it slowly and increases the speed of the motion/movement gradually. The coaches advocating high speed swings are asking you to deny science. Don't follow this advice – it doesn't work! The student exposed to this teaching philosophy may never learn ball control.

So, what is the proper advice regarding power? It's actually quite simple – you tell the student – at each developmental stage that he/she can swing as hard as they like – provided they're convinced that the ball will go in most of the time.

In the early stages of learning you should use a great deal of feeding (i.e., dead ball work), but as soon as practical live ball (rallying) work should be introduced (See Appendix III).

Teaching "Style of Play"

Aiding your students in developing a "style" of play should be a function of their personality and strengths. For detailed information on this topic, please refer to Appendix IV. The main point to observe is to make sure you understand how the students are "psychologically wired". For instance, a tall aggressive young man or lady who likes immediate reward and likes to volley, would best be coached to take balls off the rise from the baseline, how to serve and volley and how to chip and charge on the return of serve. In other terms, they should be taught as a net rusher. Training them to be a defensive or attacking baseliner would be fruitless – as it would go against the grain of their personality. Likewise, a person who loves to hit groundstrokes, is conservative in their approach to the game and is patient, would probably best be trained as either a defensive or counterpunching baseliner.

Always, take personality into account when training a student!

The processes which underlie the learning of motor skills are much different than those associated with cognitive skills. Whether you're teaching a layup in basketball or overheard smash on a tennis court, students tend to fall into one of 3 categories.

1) **Auditory learners**: learn motor skills primarily through listening to their teachers (i.e., the spoken word)

2) **Visual learners**: learn mainly through watching skilled athletes and emulating their movement patterns

3) **Tactile learners**: must "feel" the way a movement is performed. Coaching techniques used with this type of student involve (among other methods) manipulating the student's limb(s) through the desired movement patterns(s) (i.e., coach grasps student's arm, hand, etc. and physically emulates the correct motor response).

While there are players who fall strictly into one category, in most instances, people are a "blend" of 2 or all of the learning modalities.

Taking into account these differences, I advocate one of 2 approaches in teaching tennis players:

1) You can ask the student how they feel they best learn (by sight, by listening or by feeling) and teach accordingly.

2) You teach the skills using all of the sensory inputs. That way, regardless of the students learning type, their needs are addressed.

Chapter 8

"A coach is someone who can give you correction without resentment."

John Wooden

Chapter 8: Teaching Juniors, Men and Women

Juniors

As previously mentioned, teaching is both an art and a science. The principles of great coaching and teaching have not changed over time and, in all likelihood, will not because they are based on an understanding of human nature.

Before addressing how to teach types of students (young, old – juniors, men, or women), here's good advice from one of the legendary teachers, one that I was fortunate to have been able to personally learn, from Dennis Van der Meer (co-founder of the PTR and PTR hall of fame inductee): "learn your student's names at the start of a lesson and be sure to use their names frequently!"

I firmly believe that you must, from day 1, teach juniors strong character, integrity, honesty, respect for adults, peers, and opponents, and how to recover from failure. Without these qualities, children won't grow as people, and they sure won't as athletes. It's depressing to see so many coaches in all sports today failing to teach these things!

Another concept you should teach is that following a loss, there should be no excuses! Dr. Allen Fox wrote an excellent article on this subject in 2013 titled "Producing the Next Great

Champion" (check it out at allenfoxtennis.com). I have always stressed to my students (junior and adult) that only one thing needs to be said after losing. Upon shaking hands say, "Congratulations, you played better than I did." Even after laying down the ground rules, it's likely that a few students may make excuses anyway. The most common one you'll hear is, "I played so bad." To that you can respond as I do: "How do you know that your opponent wasn't having a bad day? They may have been playing the worst they've ever played! Remember, you agreed not to make excuses. If you tried your best that's all you can do, and I'll be proud of you." Even in cases of injury, there should be no excuses after all, your student chose to play/continue the match under those circumstances. I have always admired the Aussies in this regard. Hoad, Laver, Rosewall, Newcombe, Roach, Emerson, Fraser, Stolle and Rafter – never made excuses for losses and this tradition continues to this day in Australia!

Insofar as actual teaching of the game is concerned, stress **every day,** (concurrent with acceptable technique), the importance of consistency. My good friend and colleague, Dr. David Staniford (former Head Women's Tennis coach at Marquette University), calls it "error management." I think that's a great way to put it, and when you get right down to it, there are only 2 things that you can control during practice and match play:

1) Your attitude

2) Your commitment to controlling/reducing unforced errors.

The first is obvious and the second point should be too. You can reduce unforced errors, because by definition these are errors that should not have been made!

Sadly, across the country today, I see no consistent effort to teach these things! If you do so, every day, regardless of the level of student you teach, you'll get the best out of them. Moreover, it will set you apart from your peers as a more knowledgeable coach.

Unfortunately, "first strike" tennis has been what's been shoved down the throats of both parents and kids and the results have been predictable and catastrophic. For more on this topic, see Appendix VII: We Still Need to Fix American Tennis. Developing a well-rounded game has not been the prevailing coaching philosophy for nearly 20 years now, but I see that changing. It's already started and if the trend continues, and I feel it will, America can regain the international status it had from 1920-1990. If the majority of our pros teach this way, I also see the future rosters of foreign tennis players diminishing at the collegiate level with American players occupying the line up as it used to be. These thoughts are just educated guesses, only time will tell.

As a teaching professional, you can do best by "being part of the solution" (and in the process, earn more income) by teaching **all of the strokes**. In addition, teach juniors how to execute and when to employ an underspin lob. Teach them how to lob from anywhere in the court. Encourage them to use the shot anytime they are in trouble.

Try to get your students dedicated to practicing their serves 2 times per week, (about 100 serves each time), which takes roughly 25 minutes per practice session. According to Bill Tym (an excellent teaching pro, clinician and former playing professional), only 8% of the tennis playing public does so. Also, spend 40-50% of each lesson/practice in developing mid-court and volleying skills.

Teaching juniors today poses challenges that didn't exist 20 years ago. Having taught since 1975, I see kids today and kids then as being about the same in terms of their mental, social, emotional, and physical development. It's the parents who have changed and, unfortunately, it's not been for the better. Appendix I: "Overly Involved Tennis Parents": More Common Today than in the Past, explores this issue and offers some useful advice in working with parents today.

In addition to the things covered in this article, there is also the relatively new dilemma of parents who use multiple coaches for their children. They do this in the hope that one will provide the "magic pill" to greatness. Tell parents the truth and tell them early - it rarely ever works, especially in the initial stages of learning! Even if the student received identical advice (which will not be the case) from several coaches, it can't work because **the interpretation of the information by the student becomes problematic**. Coaches who may be saying the same thing describe points a little differently – and in the mind of a child that makes the information different!

The juniors that I have seen (even highly advanced ones) who use multiple coaches end up confused, frustrated, and rarely reach their potential. Think about it, in what other sports would our athletes be going to different clubs/sites for their development? I can't think of one! I am unaware of any player on the tour today that goes to the state of Maine part of the time for intensive coaching, to Iowa for part of the year with another coach, etc. Why don't we see that! It's because it doesn't work! These players may have several coaches on their coaching team, but that's different. In these instances, the coaches are all on the same page in terms of what they say. In the majority of cases, the coaching team travels with the player from tournament to tournament.

- How should juniors address you?

    I believe in students addressing coaches as "Mr.______", "Coach_____", or simply "Coach". This teaches juniors respect for authority and establishes the distinction between coach and student. Regardless of whether you're a high school or college coach, pro at a private club or country club, I don't advocate allowing juniors to call coaches by their first names. Ultimately, however, you'll have to make that decision.

- Make feedback meaningful for students.

  Regardless of the gender, age, or skill level of a student, be sure to give honest and accurate feedback. Do not use the word "good" by itself in lessons! This is a tip I picked up from Pete Collins, one of the 8 original PTR Master Professionals, author/creator of "Successful Doubles" and who was employed as director of tennis at the Augusta County Club for 34 continuous years. Pete's advice is to define what is meant by saying "good" with a supporting statement like, "Good – your weight transfer forward was outstanding on that shot!" I strongly urge you to follow this advice.

  Likewise, do not use positive feedback if performance is lackluster. Simply say "here's where you're going wrong" or "that's not good enough". There's no place for political correctness in coaching!

- Coaching juniors who can play:

  Once students can play, you should **strongly encourage** them to play at least 2 practice matches per week. Juniors today in the U.S. don't do this and it's resulted in a generation of kids who look great hitting the ball (due to all their drilling) but can't figure out how to win matches!

In any sport, practice should mimic competition and there should be simulated matches, games, scrimmages, meets, etc. That's one of the reasons that present day boxers couldn't compete (something that the overwhelming number of great/legendary coaches and trainers have repeatedly said) with the 1920-1970 pugilists.

As an example, take a look at the career of Rocky Marciano, the heavyweight champion of the world from 1952 – 1955. He compiled a record of 49-0 with 43 knockouts (the only undefeated heavyweight in history) in just 8 years. That's an average of over 8 fights per year! Compare this to a recent champion, Wladimir Klitchko whose record (compiled over 21 years) stands at 64-4. That's about half (3.2 fights per year to be exact) of what Rocky fought. Indeed, most fighters today enter the ring only once per year. Rocky Marciano trained using fight specific training exercises which included lots of sparring, skipping rope, throwing all manner of punches while in neck deep water, punching a specially designed 300 lb. heavy bag (all other heavyweights in history have trained with a 200 lb. heavy bag) and upwards of 15 miles road work daily.

The point here? All of the great fighters (past and present) and trainers (Ray Arcel, Teddy Atlas, Angelo Dundee, Dr. Freddie Pacheco, Freddie Roach, Cus D'Amato and Lou Duva) have picked Marciano to be among the top 3 heavyweights of all time, because he fought (competed) **often.** And so it goes with tennis. The more you practice what you'll face in competition, the better you are in competition. Science has proven this (the principle of specificity of training in motor skills) and yet all across the USA, I still see kids drilling excessively and playing very few practice matches!

Let's get back to the importance of your juniors playing 2 practices matches per week. It's important to understand (and you should explain this to your juniors) that playing in a tournament DOES NOT constitute a practice match. A practice match involves your student contacting someone to set a time/day/site to play a best 2 out of 3 set match! Juniors across the U.S. today are not doing this.

Incidentally, there is no question that the best juniors I coached during the latter 70's, 80's and early 90's (given the modern equipment) would be champions today. In my view (and that of many of my colleagues), there was a much larger pool of good match players then as compared to today (See Appendix IV: "We Still Need to Fix American Tennis")! The kids of the 1970's, 80's and early 90's played far more practice matches, were tougher, more independent and, in my opinion, better at recovering (i.e., rebounding) from a loss. The kids today, <u>could</u> be just as good if they'd play more practice matches.

Another topic for discussion regards junior students who are ready to "move on". If you feel that you no longer can advance a student (and in your opinion, they are still capable of improving), don't hesitate to refer them to a qualified pro who can help. Do not feel that you've failed. To the contrary, you've succeeded! You did the hard work. You brought them through the tough times. You taught them a game they love! Just be honest and tell them you are recommending a change because you care about them and want to see them continue to improve. You just feel another specialist is needed. Doctors refer their patients to specialists all the time, why should it be different in our profession? The student and his/her parents will respect you for it and they will refer other business your way.

I have seen numerous cases of pros over the years who have held onto students far too long. In the overwhelming majority of these cases, the parents changed coaches anyway and the situation ended badly with one or both parties having hurt feelings. On the other hand, I don't ever recall seeing a referral to another teacher ending awkwardly.

It is <u>extremely</u> important that you attend your student's tennis matches whenever possible. Many tennis pro's today – particularly the young ones (under 45) aren't doing this! By attending matches, you are showing you care and it's absolutely necessary in order to help your students become better match players. How can you possibly do that if you don't see how they perform in competition? Can you imagine a trainer in boxing not attending his student's fights? Have you ever heard of a track coach not showing up at his runner's meets? How about the head basketball coach only making 10-20% of his team's games? Make the time to go to as many matches as possible (there is of course, a limit to what is possible). You can't ignore the membership at your club or shirk other scheduled duties. Attending matches won't bring you immediate revenue, but it will build student and parent loyalty.

Finally, **call** your students/parents on occasion. If one of them is injured, make it a point of checking up on them. Consider sending them a **handwritten** note! A little concern on your part goes a long way towards establishing your image as a top-notch teaching professional.

Men and Women

As noted earlier, at most clubs, the overwhelming majority of lessons are with juniors and women. If you fail here, particularly with the women, you might as well pack your bags.

Men, for the most part, just want a swept (clay) court, new balls and some beer. Keep the women happy and the men will be happy. In my career, I only had one club where the men were serious lesson takers. I believe that was because most of them were retired (average age 58-63).

The reasons why men don't take lessons are somewhat complicated. I believe it's related to the nature of men. Genetically, we were programmed to be problem solvers. In ancient times, men were the hunters, responsible for putting food on the table. This mindset has stayed with us into modern times. Men, for the most part, won't stop to ask directions (if lost). Here again, they try to solve the dilemma themselves. So why would tennis (another challenge), be any different? Most men feel they can just "play tennis" and they'll get better. This, of course, is wrong. They might get a little better, but not much. The majority of the time, they're simply reinforcing bad habits.

Women are completely different. They want to take lessons. That's because they are psychologically wired much different from a male. Studies have proven females to be more intuitive and conversation driven than males. Even at ages 3-5, girls tend to play in groups while "talking through" challenges while little boys are more likely to play by themselves or if engaged in group play, speak very little. These differences make females far better candidates for group instruction. Women want to know the best way of doing things. Being more intuitive, they know that an expert can provide them answers and that this is the best way of solving problems. Sorry guys, it goes back to the old hunter gatherer debate and our ancient ancestors. When tracking game, males couldn't talk, or the prey would hear and run. The females in the tribe, being responsible for gathering and the like, had to know the difference between edible and poisonous berries and green and dry wood (to this day, color blindness almost always occurs in males – a trait which hasn't been removed by natural selection). This often took a group decision; hence conversation was necessary. These differences remain in our genetic code and it's highly likely they will forever. I point out these differences for the following reasons:

1) If you're not getting many men to take lessons don't worry about it, you can't undo thousands of years of evolution.

2) No matter what club you're at, the overwhelming attendance at clinics/lessons will be women and juniors.

3) Avoid at all costs, making the women at the club mad. They will talk about you negatively and to repair the damage will take a Herculean effort. Sometimes a pro never recovers from making this mistake.

If you're wise, you'll make sure the women become your ally. Seize upon the fact that they make more willing students! Women tend to become long term students; men tend to be short term students. Men **might** take a package of 5-10 lessons, but rarely take 6 months to a year. Women want to be taught how to play better; men just want to play. One area I would advise exploring is Mixed Doubles instruction. It works at some clubs and doesn't at others.

In summary, be aware of the differences between juniors, women and men and adjust your teaching accordingly. Doing so will enhance your chances of having a long tenure at your club.

Chapter 9

"Coming together is a beginning, staying together is progress, and working together is success."

Henry Ford

"Genius is one percent inspiration and ninety-nine percent perspiration."

Thomas A. Edison

Chapter 9: Working with Owners, Managers, Boards and Tennis Committees

Working with an Owner

In some working situations, you'll be reporting to an owner. My first job as a manager/head professional involved a sole proprietorship. From December 1980 until   April of 1989, I was employed at the Staunton Racquet Club in Staunton, VA. Five years into the job the club was expanded and renamed the Staunton Racquet Club and Fitness Center.

The owner, Mr. R.R. (Jake) Smith had built the club in 1978 and he hired me (two years later) to develop a comprehensive tennis and racquetball program. The club housed 3 indoor tennis courts and 3 racquetball courts, 2 lounges and a well-stocked pro shop.

Although I had no experience in pro shop management (as well as other areas), overall, the job was an excellent one. Mr. Smith taught me a great deal about business and human nature in general. A self-made man, he had started with nothing and founded a moving company with his brother in Staunton, VA. They purchased a truck (their life's savings at the time) and began as movers. Tragically, Jake's brother was killed in a motorcycle accident. Mr. Smith persevered, eventually growing his company into the seventh largest trucking firm in the United States (Smiths Transfer Corporation).

Mr. Smith was a firm, but fair employer and although I was young (27), he respected my opinion, especially as it related to human relations and program design. As I would come to find out later, dealing with a sole owner had many advantages over being employed at clubs with boards and general managers (and a few disadvantages),

For one thing, if I was trying to get something approved, I only had one person to convince. Secondly, and this was generally true of the older generation of millionaires – if you ran into financial difficulty – either with the business or personally – things are "fixed" immediately. Anytime we had a major heating, air conditioning or plumbing problem, all I had to do was pick up the phone and call a repairman. Everyone knew Jake and they would come right away, sometimes within the hour!

On a personal note – and outside of my immediate family, no one knows this – Mr. Smith saw to it that I was able to buy my first home. Since one of his stipulations in accepting the job was to live in Staunton (I had to move from Harrisonburg, VA, which was 18 miles north of Staunton), he set me up to rent a nice cape cod home just 600 yards from the club. We liked it so much that after eighteen months we decided to try and buy it. Unfortunately, we didn't have the money for the down payment ($4,000) and neither did our families. When Mr. Smith heard about it (he had known the seller since childhood), he called me in to his office and presented me with a $4,000 check ($10,000 in today's money). He told me that it was a loan and that I could pay it back, interest free, on my own terms!

Two years later, I was called by the manager of another club and offered a job as director of tennis at his facility. I said that I'd have to think about it and after several days, decided to accept it. I went to Mr. Smith first and told him of my decision. His response was: "have you already given your word to him?" I said I hadn't called him back with my decision. Mr. Smith then said: "Then I have a counteroffer. If you give me your word that you'll stay for at least 5 more years, you won't have to repay the $4,000 house loan and I'll give you a $3,000 raise/year (roughly $8,000 in today's money)". Needless to say, I stayed. Mr. Smith asked that I tell no one, and I didn't. I only share this now because Mr. Smith passed away 20 years ago and his wife, Doris joined him in August of 2015.

What's to be learned from this story?

1) It's an example of qualities that will benefit you as a professional. You must have integrity – your word, once given should hold true. Even if circumstances change, and you may be at a disadvantage because of it, you need to keep your word. I see this in very short supply today among many pros. The good ones do keep their word!

2) This story illustrates the biggest advantage in working with an owner. If I had been working for a board/committee/GM/or corporation, I would never have been offered a loan for my first house.

There are a few other advantages to working for an owner. Meetings are more easily arranged and they're usually short and often immediately productive. In contrast, meetings at clubs which are owned by the membership, or a corporation, have committees. Meetings with committees (which have multiple members) are more difficult to arrange and rarely is there 100% attendance. These meetings can also be inordinately long with some members pontificating over minor (or already decided) issues.

Working for clubs with boards and committees do, however, have some advantages over a sole proprietorship, principally:

1) If your position is in peril – there is strength in numbers. All you need to do to keep your job is to get support from the right committee member(s). If you lose an owner's support, you're gone no matter what!

2) Committees/boards are usually very effective in marketing you and the club's programs.

3) Committees/boards will generally be more involved in helping you out with "unreasonable" members.

Committees and Boards

"A rhinoceros was the outcome of a committee who was given the task of designing a horse."

Author unknown

Tennis committees are only as good as the members serving on them. For the most part, I had very good ones and so did most of the pros I talked to.

Boards, however, can be a different matter. Boards have more members than committees and therefore, the chances of divergent views are increased. In talking to pros about their experiences, a common theme kept coming up. Every 5-7 years, most pros reported having 1 or 2 people added to boards whose views were not in the best interests of the club. The kind of member(s) who'd come up with an idea like, "Let's save $30,000 in the budget by eliminating the tennis pros salary. He gets lesson income, right?" Every tennis pro who's been in the business for 10 years or longer can relate a similar story. Sooner or later, everyone, and you'll be no exception, runs into a board member who's "out to get tennis."

My advice in these matters is to "weather the storm." Board members have finite terms, and, in most cases, the problematic ones end up losing credibility with their fellow board members. The only thing you can do is to continue performing the duties listed in your job description to the best of your ability and wait them out.

Your tennis committee chairman should be your ally. Communicate often with him/her and keep him/her abreast of what's going on – good and bad. In the rare instance where you have a bad one, (they come in 2 forms: the overly involved/intrusive or not involved enough type) find a way to work with them. Their terms are usually short, so – like I said before: "Weather the storm!"

Working with General Managers (GM's)

In today's club environment, the average length of employment for a GM is roughly 4 years. Sadly, it's about the same for a tennis professional. The causes for this are multi-faceted but one of the primary reasons is that the new generation of young adults/parents who are joining clubs tend to be more demanding, want immediate results, are less tolerant of mistakes and overall are much more difficult to satisfy than their counterparts of just a decade earlier.

To achieve long term success, you must be able to get along with your GM. Be sure to be on time to all staff meetings and keep him/her abreast of any trouble situations that arise. No manager enjoys being "blindsided" by his members. The better the relationship with your GM, the easier your job will be. In the event you have a poor manager, and they're out there, just do everything you can to get along with him/her. If it's an untenable situation, then confide in your tennis committee chairman and get their advice.

Illustrative of this are the experiences of a friend of mine. For eight years, he had been happily employed as the director of tennis at a well-known country club in the states. The club had just lost an excellent GM who was replaced by a person whose management style was the polar opposite. This new manager had inherited a staff of seasoned professionals, yet he tried to micromanage every aspect of the club's operations. A particularly troubling practice of his was to give an employee a directive or approval for some action or idea, and if it failed, he'd lie and say it wasn't his idea or that approval was never given in the first place! This happened to my friend, who in turn reported it to his tennis committee chairman (who was also a board member). It took about eighteen months for the board to verify that this was a recurring situation, and the GM was fired.

The point here is that if you have a bad GM, do everything you can to work with him/her but keep detailed notes (with dates/times of your conversations) and seek help from your tennis committee chairman if it's necessary.

Chapter 10

"Success in life, in anything, depends upon the number of persons
that one can make himself agreeable to."

Thomas Carlyle

"The secret of many a man's success in the world resides in his insight
into the moods of men and his tact in dealing with them."

J.G. Holland

Chapter 10: Problem Members, Students, Peers and Staff

Problem Members

Clubs are a microcosm of society. The vast majority of members are good people. A smaller proportion are exceptional people, and a very small minority are difficult to deal with. Sometimes, its four or five and sometimes it's only one or two, but every club has its share of completely unreasonable people. My advice is to learn who they are as soon as possible when you start at a new club.

Rule # 1 in dealing with a problem member is: Do not try to figure out why they are as they are. This is a futile task. Perhaps their spouse ran away with a tennis pro, maybe you remind them of an abusive boyfriend or girlfriend, or perhaps they're the type of person who isn't happy unless they're complaining. It could be they just don't like you. There's only one thing you can do in dealing with these people – **kill them with kindness**! Unfortunately, there are some people who don't like the way the sun comes up in the morning. As hard as it may be, you must treat them no different than any other member. No matter how ridiculous their complaint/criticism may be, you must give it some credence. A simple statement like: "I'll check on that for you", or "I'll take that under advisement", "thanks for the suggestion" or "I'll bring that up at the next tennis committee meeting" usually appeases them. What you cannot do is say "yes" to changing something that's not within your authority to change. For instance, let's say your problem member is angry about having to pay a guest fee which is a club policy. You cannot give in and violate the club policy. Just say: "I understand how you feel, but I'm not authorized to waive the guest fee, I'll be happy to have the tennis committee and manager review the policy at the next tennis committee meeting."

To reiterate, don't waste your time trying to figure out these people and don't worry about them not liking you. Mean spirited people are everywhere, but thankfully they're in the minority. **Never** try to combat them verbally or put them down (even though they may deserve it), that just makes things worse, and it could get you fired.

Problem Students

Kids essentially are kids. I see no difference between the children of the 1970's and now, insofar as their physical and mental development are concerned. Children want rules and order and as their tennis professional you are obligated to provide that. Therefore, when they break your rules (e.g., cheating, poor court behavior, disrespect, breaking clinic rules), there must be consequences. Call their parents and let them know of your decision. Do not let bad behavior continue, if left unchecked it'll get worse. You are a teacher and it's your job to instill/teach good character, honesty, integrity, courage, self-reliance, independence and how to recover from failure.

Problem Peers and Staff

This is a no-brainer. Talk to the peer or staff member first. If this fails, see their immediate supervisor for help.

If the staff member's (and I'm talking about a staff member in another department) behavior does not affect your job performance or your members, do not be concerned, let the GM deal with the situation.

Chapter 11

"You don't drown by falling in the water; you drown by staying there."

Edwin Lewis Cole

"The problem is not that there are problems. The problem is expecting otherwise and thinking that having problems is a problem."

Theodore Rubin

Chapter 11: Customer/Club Issues

In this chapter, I cover a wide range of challenging situations, some of which are personal experiences and some of which have happened to other pros. In each case, a solution is provided. Understand that this list is by no means a complete representation of problems that can occur at clubs. Rather let it serve as a guide in the process of effective problem solving.

1. **Becoming "friends" with the members.**

   Don't do this! As the member's tennis professional, you are their teacher/organizer, nothing more! If you befriend some, it will backfire sooner or later, members will talk about it, and many will resent it. Lots of pros have lost jobs over this one!

2. **Attending member's private parties.**

   From time-to-time members will invite you to their private parties. In my opinion, you should decline the invitation and here are my reasons:

a. If you attend some and not others, regardless of your reason, the member(s) hosting the parties you couldn't attend could feel slighted.

b. If alcohol is being served, you'll probably be expected to drink, but how much? If someone thinks you're having too much to drink, then you become a topic for later conversation. Remember this, **in the club business, perception is reality!**

c. Once at the party, you'll feel as if you've returned to work. In order to make conversation, the members will bring up club related issues and you'll be forced to respond. The members don't do it to be mean spirited, it's the only thing they can talk about because they don't have any interaction with you other than when they see you at work. What else could they talk about?

d. If you don't get around to talk to everyone, some members may be offended.

e. Its fine (and recommended) to attend club sponsored parties – just avoid the private events.

3. Nepotism

Hiring a family member to work in the tennis department CAN work. I've seen it over the years and in about half the cases it did work out. My gut feeling here is you're better off hiring someone other than a relative, but that's your call.

4. Dating member/affairs

It's disturbing that I have to list this one, but the practice of dating members/having affairs is so common today that I feel I have to weigh in on the subject. In one area of the country that I am familiar with there have been 15 incidents (9 within the last 4 years) within a 50-mile radius! In every case it's involved a pro under 40 years of age!

Let's take the first situation – it's not quite as fatal as the latter (an affair). Dating a club member, no matter how much you are smitten by them, is a definite NO! Why? Because if you break up, even if it's not your fault, the members will blame you – you'll be the "bad guy". This can affect your employment stability.

Having an affair with a married member will GUARANTEE your termination and it could end your career as a tennis professional altogether. Incidentally, **never** hire an assistant or head pro who has had an affair at a club, they will do it again!

5. Member is infatuated with you

This is basically the same as the preceding situation. Ignore any advance from a member. If this fails to stop the behavior, confide in the general manager or your tennis committee chairman.

6. Members (or committee) try to determine pro's lesson rates/fees

This happened to a friend of mine about 20 years ago. Let's call him Bob (not his real name). Bob was at a point where he needed to raise some of his fees in order to offset costs. In order to justify a moderate increase in the per member charge for these clinics, Bob did a survey of what the other area clubs charged for their team clinics. As it turned out, his fee was reasonable. In spite of the survey, the ladies at the club were mad. They didn't want to pay any extra amount. Wisely, Bob let the tennis committee handle the matter and everything worked out fine.

7. Member is late for lessons

If they are perpetually late, just give them the time left on the lesson and charge them for the full time. The first time they are late, give them the full hour/time if you can. Do not, however, infringe on someone else's lesson time!

If a member repeatedly fails to show for a lesson speak to them (face to face) and explain that you can't hold the spot for them if they continue missing. Be sure to document each occurrence and let your GM and/or tennis committee chairman know. Charging them for a missed lesson is up to you – personally, I rarely did, because in most cases, the customer usually had an emergency. In rare instances, where a member is repeatedly late or fails to show, you might have to cease giving them lessons. I would only do this if all other measures had failed.

8. Trading lessons for clay court maintenance or other tennis department work

I wouldn't do it. I've done it twice in my career and it didn't work out either time.

Deciding to trade out labor for lessons usually involves using a teenager (most often for clay court maintenance). The concept is a good one - you're teaching them good character, self-reliance, etc., but it's one of those situations that's great in theory and short on results. First, the teenager has no "skin in the game". Anytime he/she is tired, has too much schoolwork, etc., they're tempted to, and usually do, miss work. They're not being paid, and their parent, in all likelihood won't get on them about not showing up. Meanwhile, you get the member complaints.

It's better to hire adults. Retired people who know something about clay court work are preferred but if that isn't possible, find someone who enjoys gardening. I've found these people easy to train, and usually detailed oriented. They're also used to manual labor, and they take pride in their work.

9. Collecting guest fees

If your club has a guest fee policy, be sure to enforce it. I've seen lots of pros get in trouble for failing to collect guest fees or worse, selectively enforcing the policy.

10. Professional courtesy to visiting pros.

Most clubs do not charge a guest fee to a visiting club pro. If your club doesn't have such a policy, I suggest you bring it up with your tennis committee.

11. Accepting tips

When someone offers a tip, I advise accepting it (humbly of course).

You can always say "Well that's not necessary", (but do accept it). Why? The person obviously has the disposable income to do so, and it makes them feel good to do so.

12. "Special rates" for certain students

Although I have done this and have known others to do so, in most cases, I advise against it. Even if you insist that the customer keep the arrangement secret, sooner or later it'll get out, and then you've got problems.

There is one exception that I'd make - if someone (mother or father) loses their job. In most of these cases it's their child that's taking the lessons. I only charge half price until the parent secures employment. I also let them know they don't need to pay me back. Additionally, I ask that they don't tell the child and that payment be sent in a sealed envelope. Showing compassion in such a case is the right thing to do and although you'll lose money in the short term, you'll gain business in the long run.

13. Teaching children who have little or no interest in tennis

These situations are tough but require honesty on your part. If you are convinced that a child has no interest in learning the game, let the parent(s) know. Tell them the truth - that no pro can coach "desire" or "a love of the game." To continue would not be fair to them or the child. Do mention that you have seen cases where children age a couple of years and decide they want to play and that if this happens, you'll be glad to take them as students again.

14. Multiple bosses

Having more than one boss cannot work. Do not accept a job where this is the case. Ask for a written job description when interviewing for a position. A well written job description should clearly define who you report to. If the job doesn't have a job description, what does this tell you?

15. Ladies want the pro to choose their partners and/or determine their line up for league play.

Do not do this under any circumstances! Tell the ladies that you are their coach/teacher, that you're there to help them play better and that it's up to them to choose their own partner. Explain that it's up to them to determine their line up (i.e., which player plays #1, which player plays #2 etc.). Suggest that they use a challenge ladder to verify the positions. If this fails, and it probably will (women are notoriously reluctant to using challenge ladder play), appoint a team captain whose responsibility (among other things) is to determine the lineup.

16. Overly involved parent wants to be present at a child's private lesson

Deciding whether to permit a problematic parent to attend their child's lesson should be a function of how distracting they are to you and/or the child. If it's a matter of them asking an occasional question that's one thing. If, however, they try to tell you how to coach, then they should be banned from attending. Only in rare instances should a parent be allowed inside the fence (i.e., on the court) for a lesson.

If you do have to ban a parent from lessons, be sure to do it diplomatically. Explain to the parent that you need the full attention of their child during lessons and that isn't possible if they are present.

Chapter 12

"If a man empties his purse into his head no one can take it from him. An investment in knowledge always pays the best interest."

Benjamin Franklin

"Unless you do something beyond what you've already mastered, you will never grow."

Ronald E. Osborne

Chapter 12: Growing in Your Profession

I've always viewed improvement as a player and teacher as an on-going process. In my opinion, the only way of improving at anything is by becoming a lifelong learner.

One day I had a conversation with a good friend of mine, Art Abbott of Charlotte, North Carolina, who is a seasoned tennis professional on this topic. Art's resume is exceptional. He began teaching in 1972. He served as the head tennis professional at Old Providence Racquet Club (Charlotte, NC) for 9 years and following that, 10 years as head tennis professional at Quail Hollow Country Club in Charlotte! Art then ran the tennis program at Park Crossing in Charlotte for 10 years. Additionally, he served as the head men's tennis coach at UNCC and was voted "Coach of the Year" for the sunbelt conference in 1985. Now, at the age of 67, he's still teaching privately, is a successful high school tennis coach and is a certified referee for both ITA and USTA tennis matches/tournaments. Art's thoughts on becoming a lifelong learner in tennis were quite insightful: "A huge part of being a great teaching professional is attitude. Being on time, doing everything professionally, having a highly positive attitude, being organized, and planning ahead of time. Attitude also extends to staying abreast – constantly, of ways to do your job better. Today, with the teaching organizations and the internet, there are limitless opportunities to better your teaching and programming skills. I've always felt that when you stop trying to improve, you start falling behind. Even today, I strive to get better, to find new ways to get better, to find new ways of helping players improve."

There's one goal that I would add for today's teaching pro - to attend your organizations (PTR, USPTA) yearly symposium. There's just no excuse for not making the time to do so. Most clubs will pay for it, and it helps to "recharge" one's batteries! I have attended all but four PTR International Symposia since I was certified in 1982 and at each, I came away with at least two good ideas. In addition to the yearly symposium, PTR offers a number of specialty courses and additional certifications.

Do not follow in the footsteps of so many pros that I see today who simply rest on their laurels. You must constantly strive all of your working life to improve. In the words of the great boxing trainer Ray Arcel: "To rest is to rust."

Chapter 13

"The first wealth is health"

Ralph Waldo Emerson

"A feeble body weakens the mind."

John – Jacques Rousseau

"True enjoyment comes from the activity of the mind and exercise of the body; the two are ever united."

Willhelm von Humbolt

Chapter 13: Staying in Shape

I. Physical Health

I hear it often that being a tennis pro is a young man's job. There is some truth to this statement if you're going to rely on just your job duties to keep you in shape. Without question, you've got to exercise in order to achieve longevity as a teaching professional.

Before discussing the specific exercise activities I'd advocate, certain facts regarding aging must be kept in mind:

1) Starting around age 40, if you don't strength train, you'll lose approximately 1% of your body strength per year (hence, if you do nothing, you'll be 20% weaker at age 60 than you were at age 40). After 60 it can accelerate to 3% loss per year. This is true for both of the sexes, but the decrement in females is much more noticeable since they have only about 50%-65% of the upper body strength of a male (so a female's bottom end for upper body strength is much lower than a males).

2) If you begin strength training (and it doesn't have to be that much) at age 40 or earlier, the decrement in strength loss can be reduced to roughly .1% per year.

3) There is only one parameter of fitness that does not have to decrease with age – flexibility. Since males from early childhood on are far less flexible than females, it is

highly recommended that minimal flexibility training be adopted by all male tennis professionals.

4) Research clearly supports the contention that longevity, quality of life, mental health and stress reduction are improved through regular exercise.

To most, it would appear that a tennis pro gets all of the exercise that s/he needs through daily work activity, but this isn't the case. The work being performed is repetitive in nature – certain muscles are worked, and others are not. Moreover, a great deal of time, depending on the cross section of your clients, can involve standing. It is, therefore, prudent to have a regular strength training regimen which targets the primary movements used in the performance of your work.

Gray Cook (arguably today's preeminent sports and orthopedic physical therapist) and I have written two books (Power, Speed and Stamina for Tennis (1998) and Functional Tennis Training (Release Date - 2023) which address many of these topics. For the upper body, we recommend the Chop and Lift exercises and for the lower limbs, the assisted (for older pros) and resisted forward lunge (all exercises use elastic tubing). These exercises should be performed two times per week for most of the year. For complete information on these and other specific exercises, please refer to either of the aforementioned books or go to Gray's website: www.functionalmovementsystems.com.

The entire upper body workout takes no more than twenty-five to thirty minutes (two times per week). So, for an investment of about an hour each week, you can significantly improve your ability to perform your job (and play tennis)! Since your dominate elbow undergoes considerable stress on a daily basis, we also recommend a few supplementary exercises for the forearm(s). These are detailed in Appendix V ("Preventing Tennis Elbow"). If time is an issue and you had to select only one of these activities in this article, then stick to the rubber band exercise.

Regardless of your age, a few other things can help make your job easier:

1) If you have a long teaching day, reserve time to get a shower and change into fresh clothes and socks.

2) If you can't take a shower, change shirts and socks often.

3) Especially in the summer, seek out shade whenever you can – the sun is tough on the skin and robs you of energy.

4) Sit down when you can (e.g., when students are involved in match play), but make sure you're involved in the coaching process. Sitting down saves a great deal of energy and there's nothing wrong with it as long as you're attentive to the needs of

the student(s). I once worked for a guy who didn't want any of his pros sitting down – ever. After explaining to him that coaches in other sports sit down (ex. basketball, baseball, etc.), he changed his mind,

5) Always wear a hat outside (broad circular brims are the best because they shield the ears and neck.) Wearing a hat lowers scalp/head temperature by roughly 15 degrees.

6) Always wear sunglasses outside. I failed to do so for the first fifteen years of my career. This resulted in my developing a cataract in my left eye, which was corrected through surgery. Get a good pair, such as Oakley's or other brands that block UVB and UVA rays.

7) Use sunscreen every day.

8) Avoid (especially as you get older) booking a lot of back-to-back lessons. Stay in air conditioning in between lessons.

9) Know your limits and pace yourself. Don't book so many lessons in a day that by the time you get to the last student you're unable to give a quality lesson.

10) Don't skip meals, especially lunch.

II. Mental Health

Certain professions, and tennis is one of them, have a higher incidence of depression. The reasons why this is so, are multifaceted. Factors such as a) high stress   (more prevalent in jobs which involve dealing with the public), b) long hours, c) lack of sleep, d) having a people pleasing personality, e) being worn out physically, f) being too much of a perfectionist or g) the experience of having had a catastrophic personal event (e.g., death of a loved one), can all be contributing factors.

Being aware of the warning signs of the disease can, quite literally be crucial to your survival. Depression is a very serious disease, as real as cancer, diabetes, gout or any other malady, and left untreated can totally debilitate a person. Some of the warning signs of depression include:

1) Failing to enjoy activities that once gave you pleasure.

2) A profound sense of sadness or hopelessness that lasts several months or longer.

3) Lake of confidence in the performance of one's job duties.

4) Lack of energy.

5) Insomnia or on the other hand, sleeping too much.

6) Persistent thoughts of suicide.

7) Loss of appetite or eating too much.

8) Inability to concentrate/inability to make decisions. Even the simplest decisions seem incredibly difficult.

9) A dread of interacting with people.

Depression, like some other diseases (e.g., heart disease, alcoholism, cancer) tends to run in families, so there is probably a genetic link. I have suffered from depression three times in my life – one short bout and two very long bouts, and I can honestly say it was awful, particularly the last 2 bouts. No words can describe the panic, helplessness and sense of hopelessness that I experienced. In my case, it was hereditary/biochemical. There was a long generational history of depression on both sides of my family.

So, what should you do if you are depressed? Seek immediate help! Start with your family physician – he'll probably refer you to a psychologist or psychiatrist. Be sure to take medication if it's prescribed and take it for the length of time recommended. There's nothing to be ashamed of in having to take antidepressants, many people have experienced depression or have had someone in their family who has been affected. It may be that, like me, you'll have to take the medication long term – perhaps the rest of your life. Realize that finding a medication that works best for you is a trial-and-error process (it usually takes 2-3 weeks for an antidepressant to properly work). Be patient, if one doesn't work, know that there's one that will, and your doctor will find it.

If you are depressed, I would confide in your GM or immediate supervisor and let him/her know what you're going through. Most employers will be very sympathetic to your situation and allow for a medical leave of absence if it's necessary.

There are any number of great books on the subject, but one that I highly endorse is Cliff Ritchie's (a former #1 U.S. player) first-hand account battling the disease titled: <u>Acing Depression: A Tennis Champions Toughest Match.</u> 1

In summary, if you develop depression, seek qualified medical help. Try to force yourself to go to work. You'll usually feel better as the day wears on and be sure to get regular exercise. It will eventually go away, and you'll be good as new, maybe even better!

A final point on mental health: get in the habit of resting on your designated days off. Do not go back to your place of work for any reason.

There is a tendency, especially among young pros, to "burn the candle at both ends". I have seen this occur in 2 situations: 1) where the pro has a personality where he/she finds it difficult to say "no", and 2) where a pro is making a good income. In the latter case, these pros just can't leave well enough alone, they teach every clinic and lesson that comes their way. It's as if they've become addicted to money. This can be a terrible mistake. As with any job, the wise tennis professional should balance hard work with time off. Why? The answer should be obvious. Jobs which demand working with the public involve periods of high stress. Prolonged stress combined with being physically tired can lead to burnout, or worse, failing health. Additionally, a pro who becomes a workaholic can find his/her family life suffering. I have seen too many cases of divorce resulting from pros not being able to pry themselves away from their club!

As the old saying goes" "take time to smell the roses, or you'll soon be pushing them up!"

Chapter 14

"I'm a coach because of the kids and the passion I have for the game and sport itself. There is no better feeling than teaching a child the importance of discipline, hard work, effort, dedication, determination and the heart it takes to win not only in sports but in life."

Bill Pingitor

"A coach is someone who tells you what you don't want to hear, who has you see what you don't want to see, so that you can be who you have always known you could be."

Tom Landry

Chapter 14: What about High School or College Coaching?

Coaching college tennis can be very rewarding, but it's a completely different job than that of a tennis professional. In general, it involves far less teaching and a greater time investment in managing people. Recruiting players that are already good is about 70% of the secret to coaching college tennis. A great deal of the collegiate coach's job is also spent in ensuring that his/her players are/stay eligible to play. Unless you're at a large Division I program, a substantial amount of time will also be spent with fundraising. Tennis budgets, particularly at most Division II and III schools, are woefully lacking.

Collegiate Coaching in Conjunction with Club Work

Combining collegiate coaching with employment at a club can be a win-win situation. Being permitted to do this (by the GM and board) requires excellent administrative and planning skills and the understanding that the member's needs always come first.

I was the men's and women's head coach at Catawba College (Division II) in Salisbury, NC from 1998-2004. At the same time, I served as the head tennis professional at the Country Club of Salisbury. The situation worked out great – I became busy with the college when the country club program was winding down (Fall) and when the Spring season for collegiate play was completed in May, the club was getting busy. I was able to get the support of the tennis committee and they presented it, with their endorsement, to the board. Since I had been doing a good job for the club for 8 years, the board had no problem in approving it.

College Coaching as a Career

If you're considering college coaching as a career, here are some things to keep in mind:

a) At all but the largest (mostly Division I schools) the pay isn't very good. You can make an income off of summer camps, but even this is limited if you're employed at a school with poor name recognition.

b) At many schools, the AD's focus is on the revenue sports with the non-revenue sports taking a back seat. They just don't want any trouble from the players on your team(s). A case in point: I had a friend, we'll call him Roger, who was the head men's and women's tennis coach at a Division II school. His women's team won the conference in his first year as a coach. He gave his AD the championship trophy to be displayed along with the football, and basketball trophies. Four weeks passed and the trophy hadn't been put in the case, so the coach asked about it. The AD said he'd get right on it. He didn't. To cut a long story short Roger had to ask four more times before the trophy was displayed. It took 3 months to do what amounted to unlocking a glass case! Think this AD cared about the program? Incidentally, the AD hardly ever showed up at a match, but he was waiting in the coach's office anytime something went wrong (e.g., a kid getting a DWI, etc.).

c) The budget for most college tennis programs is inadequate.

d) You'll be on the road (having to go out of town) for about 50% of your schedule.

e) Depending on the school, college coaching can be an unstable employment situation. Unfortunately, it's not uncommon today to see a college drop their tennis program. While this is much more common with men's programs, I have seen women's teams dropped as well. Think about it – if a school is trying to determine how to cut expenses, the quickest and least painful way for the AD to do it is by dropping tennis scholarships which effectively kills the program. There aren't that many (irate) parents to deal with, most of the alumni won't care or will get over it quickly and the school can slash $60,000 -$100,000 in expenses.

Unless a college can combine coaching with a teaching position, I'd strongly recommend that you also keep your job as a pro at a club. That way, if college coaching doesn't work out (or vice versa) you'll still have a job.

Coaching at a high school can be very rewarding and it can result in future lessons and camps, but it pays very little. If you do the math, it's not uncommon to see compensation in the range of $2-$4/hour. Like college coaching, consider combining this with a club job.

Have a good relationship with middle school/high school coaches

If you're a club pro (and don't coach school tennis) make sure to build a good relationship with the area high school and middle school coaches. Most of these coaches don't have much experience and they do the best they can, given their busy daily teaching schedule. So, present yourself as a potential aid, not an adversary. Under no circumstances (and I've seen this happen too often) should you denigrate their efforts to the parents or players. If a parent comments "the coach doesn't know what he/she's doing" just say "I'll see if I can help out."

Chapter 15

"By failing to prepare, you are preparing to fail."

Benjamin Franklin

"It's better to look ahead and prepare, than to look behind and regret."

Jakie Joyner-Kersee

Chapter 15: Preparing for the Future

A tennis professional's longevity is largely a function of having the right kind of position at each phase of his/her career.

In the first decade of employment most pros work as assistant professionals. These positions are characterized by long hours on the court (often numerous back-to-back lessons/clinics), a substantial amount of court maintenance, stringing tennis racquets and covering the pro shop. Assistant pros often work 48-60 hours per week with only one day off. Across the country, this seems to be changing. Many clubs are now giving their pros two days off (in my opinion this is a good thing).

After a successful tenure as an assistant professional (and there is no predictable time frame for this), most pros get a chance to move up to a head pro or director's job. Most of these positions require long teaching hours, a great deal more responsibility and the supervision of assistant pros. These jobs can provide many satisfying years of employment, and if the pro has done a good job, stability.

At some point, usually the last decade of employment, the overwhelming majority of pros reduce the number of hours they teach. Indeed, most of their time is spent in ensuring the tennis department has qualified, committed assistant pros. A good deal of time is also spent in mentoring these pros to become better at what they do. The Director's teaching is, in many cases, reserved for special clinics, older members and women. The pros at this stage of their career have often been at their club for eight to twelve years.

If you are at this stage of your career and are looking for a new job, expect it to take a while. You can get a new job at age 55 to 60, but it will, in all likelihood have to be a club with an older membership (55+).

Chapter 16

"The trouble with new books is they prevent you from reading the old ones."

John Wooden

"If we encounter a man of rare intellect, we should ask him what books he reads."

Ralph Waldo Emerson

Chapter 16: The Best Tennis Books

The value of a book is, of course, specific to its subject matter. The following is a list of books which have helped me grow as a teacher. There are many other fine works, and, without doubt, others will be written in the future. This list covers a variety of topics and each one provides unique insights. They are discussed in no particular order.

1) <u>Match Play & the Spin of the Ball</u> (1929) (Bill Tilden):

This is, what I consider, the finest book ever written on tennis. It's simply amazing that it was published in 1929. The fact that 90% of what Tilden has to say regarding tactics/shot selection holds up today is testimony to his genius. It's out of print, so you'll have to get it through interlibrary loan.

2) <u>Fundamentals of Tennis</u> (1970) (Stanley Plagenhoef)

Another classic. Stanley Plagenhoef was a highly successful tennis coach and professor at Wesleyan University. He was the first and arguably the most prolific tennis researcher. Everything in this slim (117 pages) body of work has stood the test of time.   You'll have to get this through interlibrary loan.

3) <u>The Game of Singles in Tennis</u> (1968) (Bruce Old, Bill Talbert)

4) <u>The Game of Doubles in Tennis</u> (1968) (Bruce Old, Bill Talbert)

The above two books represent the most exhaustive undertaking to date in the area of strategy and tactics. Both Talbert and Old hand charted hundreds of professional matches in order to determine percentage tactics for baseline play, serving, returning, approach shots, net play, overhead smash and a host of other game specific situations. They are out of print, but both are available through interlibrary loan.

5) <u>If I'm the Better Player, Why Can't I Win?</u> (1979), (Dr. Allen Fox)

6) <u>Think to Win: The Strategic Dimension of Tennis</u> (1993), (Dr. Allen Fox)

7) <u>The Winner's Mind: A Competitor's Guide to Sports and Business Success</u> (2005)

8) <u>Tennis: Winning the Mental Match</u> (2010), (Dr. Allen Fox)

I can't say enough great things about the work of Dr. Allen Fox. He is in my opinion, in a class by himself for one simple reason: most everything written in the abovementioned four books could apply to a 3.0 or 7.0 level tennis player. More than any other author past or present, he has helped me grow, both as a player and coach! Go to Allen's website to order. (allenfoxtennis.com)

9) <u>World Class Tennis Technique</u> (2001) (Paul Roetert and Jack Groppel editors).

A very complete and sound work on virtually every aspect of the game. Twenty-eight authors with backgrounds ranging from former world class players to national coaches weigh in on everything from technique to footwork and strength training. The sequence photographs, in particular, are excellent.

10) <u>Maximum Tennis: 10 Keys to Unleashing Your On-Court Potential</u> (2002) (Nick Saviano)

A master professional with both the USPTA and PTR, Saviano competed successfully on the ATP tour for 9 years and had wins over numerous top 10 players. Additionally, he was formerly the director of coaching education for the USTA. A very complete and insightful work, for both players and coaches!

11) <u>Power, Speed and Stamina for Tennis: A Complete Guide for the Player and Coach</u> (1999) (Gray Cook and Jack Thompson)

A pragmatic guide to tennis specific strength training and conditioning. The book details the supporting research for using PNF exercise, low level plyometrics and interval training for tennis players. Pre and post test procedures and specific on and off court drills/exercises are also covered in detail. It's out of print, so you'll have to go through interlibrary loan.

12) <u>Athletic Body In Balance</u> (2003) (Gray Cook)

A comprehensive guide on how to train athletes for smooth, fluid movement and how to prevent muscle imbalances, mobility restrictions, stability problems and injuries. Quite literally, this work set into motion the international movement towards functional training.

13) <u>Functional Tennis Training</u> (Release date Winter, 2023, Gray Cook and Jack Thompson) eBook available through Thompson tennis.net and FunctionalMovementSystems.com, as well as your favorite online bookseller.

Picks up where our 1999 book left off. In addition to new tennis specific exercises and drills, there is a wealth of information on periodization training and the importance of functional movement screen testing for tennis players.

14) <u>Natural Tennis (2nd addition)</u> (2010) (David Staniford and John Boaz).

The authors demonstrate how the principles of natural movement can be applied to tennis coaching and training. This book emphasizes the role of body awareness and space awareness and how these concepts improve error management. There is also a thorough discourse on percentage tactics for singles and doubles.

15) <u>From Breakpoint to Advantage: A Practical Guide to Optimal Tennis Health and Performance</u> (2004) (Babette Pluim and Marc Safran)

An excellent reference book for injury prevention and treatment of/ rehabilitation of injuries. The book covers training programs for flexibility, balance, stabilization and strength, proper nutrition and equipment selection. In addition, the authors discuss the considerations coaches should give to working with different aged students (e.g., juniors, vets, women and wheelchair athletes) as well as other issues including overtraining, doping and traveling.

16) <u>Tennis Training: Enhancing On-Court Performance</u> (2007) (Dr. Mark Kovacs, W. Britt Chandler, Dr. T. Jeff Chandler).

A superb book in all respects. The science supporting exercises for tennis is presented in a way that all coaches and pros can understand, and the photographs of the training activities are excellent. This is definitely one you should have in your library. Written by three of the most respected authors/clinicians in the field.

17) <u>Mental Toughness Training for Sports: Achieving Athletic Excellence</u> (1991) (Dr. Jim Loehr).

Picking just one of Dr. Jim Loehr's works as "best" was extremely difficult. Suffice it to say that virtually everything he's ever done (books, lectures, specialty courses, etc.) has been outstanding. This is the one I first read and to this day, what I learned from it continues to help me help my students with their mental toughness.

18) <u>Tennis Practice Games</u> (2003) (Joe Dinofer)

Joe Dinofer is a PTR International Master Pro and USPTA Master Professional. An excellent speaker and clinician, he founded and is currently CEO of On Court Off Court, a company specifically dedicated to helping pros become better pros through education, teaching aids and equipment for every type of student. In my opinion this is the finest book ever written on tennis drills and practice games. What really sets it apart from other such books is the ease with which a pro can **immediately** use the information and apply it on court!

Chapter 17

"Take care of your body. It's the only place you have to live."

Jim Rohn

"If you are not your own doctor, you are a fool."

Hippocrates

Chapter 17: Items Every Pro Should Have in Their Bag, Office, or Home

1) <u>Four racquets</u> (What you are presently using). Two strung for the outdoor months (a bit tighter usually) and two strung (looser) for colder weather.

2) <u>String</u> – two to four packs of the string you currently use.

3) <u>Vibration dampeners</u> (2)- have a couple of extra dampeners in your bag (if you use them).

4) <u>Pressure wraps</u> for injuries. These can make the difference between being able to give a lesson or being sidelined. In my opinion, the best wraps on the market are manufactured by **Body Helix**, they're extremely durable and will not slip out of place. To order, visit their website (bodyhelix.com).

5) <u>Hydrocollator (Moist Heat Hot Pac)</u>: Used by physical therapists, a hydrocollator is a canvas/terry covered pack used to provide 30 minutes of moist heat (far better than electric heat) therapy. They come in 7 different sizes. The one I'd recommend is 10" X 12" as this size is adaptable to most injuries. To use, you boil it in water, then wrap it in a towel. A separate towel folded over several times is put over the injured area and the

towel wrapped Hydrocollator is placed on top of the folded towel padding the affected area. Since roughly 80% of the injuries you sustain respond to either cold or heat therapy, this is a wise investment! When the hydrocollator is not in use, it can be kept on the stove top, submerged in water, or stored in a plastic bag inside the freezer. Do not let it dry out after using it! I bought mine through Patterson Medical.

6) <u>Dixie cups</u> with frozen water (kept in freezer) for ice massage. (Ice massages should be performed for no longer than 10 minutes).

7) <u>1 large bottle</u> of Aleve (Naproxen) or Advil (Ibuprofen) or both.

8) Box of Band Aides.

9) <u>Two to Three rolls of white athletic tape.</u> For injuries and teaching applications (one example: if the student is learning a new grip and you notice they are changing back to their old one, it's sometimes necessary to tape their hand in place so they can't change it).

10) <u>Gauze pads</u>

11) <u>One small bottle of Vitamin E gel caps</u>. A pharmacist gave me this tip. If you teach outdoors during the cold months, your hands tend to chap and develop small tears (cracks). When these develop, use the "juice" from a Vitamin E gel cap on the affected area. Just use a pin or knife and cut a hole in the gel cap and squeeze the liquid into the cut. Place a band aid over the area. Be sure to do this **overnight** and if possible, during the daytime as well. Do not use "New-skin" or any other liquid bandage product, these don't work and may even make the damage worse!

12) <u>Five to Eight "Hothands" and Hot Feet" packs for the cold months</u>. As far as I'm concerned these are indispensable for the cold months. Having cold hands and feet can make teaching outdoors during the winter miserable.

13) One current copy of "<u>A Friend at Court</u>". Just in case you or someone else needs clarification on the rules.

14) <u>Chapstick</u>

15) <u>Thin gloves</u> (1 pair), Thick gloves (1 pair)

16) <u>Ankle brace</u> – three of the best on the market are the ASO brace, and the McDavid 195, and McDavid Level 3 brace.

17) If you wear <u>contacts</u>: one back-up set of contacts.

18) Thirty to fifty of your <u>business cards</u>.

19) One **<u>net center strap</u> and two to three <u>metal anchors</u>** for the center straps (these break regularly).

20) <u>A good pair of **sunglasses**</u> that provide glare protection. Oakleys, although expensive,

are hard to beat.

21) <u>Wear a **wristwatch**</u>, a cheap but reliable one, like a Timex. If you lose it, it won't matter. Do not rely on your cell phone for the time. In a recent article, Peter Burwash, a USPTA Master Professional, weighed in on this topic: "The biggest challenge today among younger professionals is their addiction to the new technology. They have become addicted to monologuing (Facebook, Twitter, etc.). They do not know how to dialogue very well, an integral part of being a great teacher. On the other hand, many of the younger generation are very bright and have a lot to contribute, if they can disconnect from their addiction of checking their phone every few minutes." Going over and picking up a cell phone to check the time makes you look like you can't wait for the lesson to be over! A wristwatch, on the other hand, can be checked when the student isn't looking.

Chapter 18

"To give real service, you must add something that cannot be bought or measured with money, and that is sincerity and integrity."

Douglas Adams

"A customer is the most important visitor on our premises, he is not dependent on us. We are dependent on him. He is not an interruption in our work. He is the purpose of it. He is not an outsider in our business. He is part of it. We are not doing him a favor by serving him. He is doing us a favor giving us an opportunity to do so."

Mahatma Gandhi

Chapter 18: Views on the Characteristics of Good Tennis Pros: What Club Members and Clients Have to Say

"What I look for in a Tennis Pro:

- Someone who will listen to what you are saying.
- Someone who will not have to win the point himself (we know he's better – that's why we are taking lessons).
- Someone who will stretch you without crushing you.
- Someone who will encourage you.
- Someone who can balance learning new skills (in your head) with learning new skills muscle wise!
- Someone who can balance feed drill with play drill.
- Someone who can tell the difference between "I just messed up this shot" and "I don't really know how to do this."
- Someone who doesn't think that just because you are older, you can't learn new things.
- Someone who teaches strategy and understanding of the game.
- Someone who shows good character and goes the extra distance to make sure his customers are happy!"

Marsha Patterson

Cabarrus Country Club
Concord, NC

"I've been a member of clubs for many years, so I've seen good tennis pros and bad ones. The best one I had was first – a good person - he was a good role model in the community. You knew he cared deeply about the club's members. He was an excellent teacher and even when you weren't taking lessons, he'd come out to watch you play – and give you feedback. You almost felt he was a member. You can't fake that kind of interest! He took pride in his work. The bad pros I've seen were all the same – lazy – didn't seem to care about the members. They'd let the assistant pro do the work while they'd be on the computer! They just weren't at the club enough."

Doug Muir

Old North State Club
New London, NC

"A good pro should:

1) <u>Have good communication skills</u>: a willingness to search for the words that will have meaning for a struggling student. He/she should also show <u>persistence</u> in communicating programs in teaching, in recruiting players and in promoting events.

2) <u>Have a comprehensive knowledge</u>: of how to execute the many variations of shots, of resources, of equipment, of physical training and minor injury treatment. He/she should also understand facility maintenance.

3) <u>Have the ability to analyze</u>, as in analyzing an individual's strokes and in how to improve those strokes in analyzing the strategy a player uses.

4) Exercise a conscientious attitude toward all aspects of the job."

Martha Smith

The Old North State Club
New London, NC

"It doesn't seem that many pros today keep up with their administrative duties. Things like showing up on time, calling members to reschedule lessons that have been cancelled due to inclement weather, and returning messages seem to take a backseat to their on-court duties. It's vitally essential for the pro to demonstrate a love for teaching all levels of players – both juniors and adults. Integrity, caring about all the members, strong character, developing boundaries to preclude romantic relationships with members are of paramount importance."

Annette Scott

Greenwood Country Club
Greenwood, SC

"The most overrated thing with teaching pros is world level playing ability. In fact, some of the worst pros I've seen over the years have been outstanding players! To me a good pro is someone who can make someone incrementally better by putting things in simple terms – who can take what the student has and "tweak" their game so that they play better. For me – I don't want to be learning a "Serena" swing volley or a "Nadal" topspin follow through. I want a pro to have excellent communication skills and I want them to care about me. I really appreciate the ones that ask me how I did in my last match. For instance, asking me if I did the things we worked on in the last lesson. The pro has to demonstrate a passion for helping everyone."

Jonathan Heard

Knoxville Racquet Club
Knoxville, TN

"One of the most important qualities I want in a pro is that he/she take a genuine interest in you as a player. They must be encouraging – while motivating you to achieve higher goals within your realistic abilities. The really bad pros I've seen attempt to coach everyone as if they're a Division I college player – they can't adapt their teaching style to accommodate and improve those with lesser capabilities. I want a pro to watch me play in matches (when they can) and to give me meaningful feedback as to how to improve. The pro must be personable and have good drills. Moreover, they must be able to explain how the drill related to playing/competing."

Wendy Fowler

Country Club of Salisbury
Salisbury, NC

"The first word that comes to mind when I think of a good tennis professional is "anticipate". He or she must be able to anticipate the needs of the membership. They must anticipate (and learn) the needs of all levels of players and be able to determine what programming activities will draw people to the club. A good pro must also address how to make things affordable for his/her clientele. Being organized and having good human relation skills – especially with the women is extremely important. Finally, I feel a good pro must understand the market of their community."

Larry Ingold

Tennis Committee member
The Old North State Club
New London, NC

Here's a comment from a colleague with a unique perspective. Angela Heider owns and operates the Lake Norman Tennis Center in Mooresville, NC. She is in the position of having to hire tennis pros and both she and her children take lessons at the club. Her insights are spot on as to what it takes to be a good tennis professional:

"In order to learn the game of tennis, a coach must have a solid, principled training method and more importantly, be able to relay information about said method efficiently and in a manner which motivates students to stay on track with making any needed changes. Of course, none of that will matter unless the coach also loves tennis, loves teaching, and truly loves to help his/her students. In order to be a productive business partner a tennis professional must also be able to organize themselves, their court and their programs, promote, and of course teach. Finally, a tennis professional must be just that – professional. They must have a moral compass and be able to abide by it and they must develop a set of off court skills that will allow them to make positive contributions both on and off court. So, in addition to continually improving on court skills, I would recommend that tennis professionals develop an off-court niche such as marketing, business management, or technology and filming."

Angela Heider

"A good tennis pro has the ability to teach the fundamentals of tennis in order to raise the level of your play. A good tennis pro is passionate about teaching!"

Carol Latimer

Country Club of Salisbury
Salisbury, NC

"Having been a member at Old Providence Racquet Club for 50 years, I've seen a number of tennis pros here and in the Charlotte area. All the really good ones had extremely good communication skills and they had good personalities. They were good role models in our community, and they all exuded a great passion for the game and teaching. They also made their programs fun and genuinely cared about the membership. Finally, they all were patient and demonstrated an extremely good work ethic."

Evelyn Hinson

Old Providence Racquet Club
Charlotte, NC

"The dedicated tennis pro must possess a number of qualities to be successful and remain in the business as a career. A tennis pro must maintain a high degree of professionalism in all aspects of their work. They must possess and develop inter-personal skills and be able to relate to people of all walks of life. This includes maintaining a professional "distance" between themselves and their clientele. The tennis professional should never show favoritism toward

116

any student or family. The tennis pro must exude passion for teaching the game and treat all students with respect, regardless of age, skill level, or coachability. In my experience, the best pros did not teach by "cookie cutter" methodology (one size fits all). The "best pros" were able to teach young, athletically gifted students one way, and could "tweak" the older established player's strokes to improve their skills and enjoyment of the game. These pros give theory and reason as to why to make a change or adjustment in a grip or stroke. Finally, just like doctors, the dedicated teaching pros constantly hone their skills as teachers by reading, going to conferences, seminars, and staying current with new ideas in the literature. This is a lifelong process and does not stop after receiving one's Tennis Pro Teaching certification."

David Skowronek

Snee Farm Country Club
Mount Pleasant, SC

"A good tennis professional is the real difference in their tennis community. They don't have to be the best player around, but they should know more about tennis than anyone if the word "professional" is attached to their name. This is what makes him or her the go-to person for all things tennis. Furthermore, the good pro establishes the tennis culture for their community. This is why some localities are called "tennis towns". The good club pro creates the environment that promotes love of the game. This only happens when the pro is totally committed to making his or her club the best around, "the place" to go if you are a tennis player. A good tennis pro is capable of being held in the same high regard as a high school football coach. But it will only happen if the pro has a strong work ethic and behaves in a fashion that makes them worthy of being called "professional."

David Flanagan

Former Head Boys and Girls
Tennis Coach Patrick Henry High School
Roanoke VA
Member of numerous clubs in VA and TN.

"I played junior and collegiate tennis and have been competing in the USTA senior division for over 7 years. In that time, I've taken lessons from all kinds of pros – old and young. The really superb teaching pros first and foremost had great personalities. There was a deep caring attitude that extended to all facets of their work – whether it was giving a lesson, talking to someone about equipment or running an event. They became the fabric of the club. They created a family atmosphere where the club was "the place" to go for tennis. You just couldn't imagine the club without them! In my opinion the most overrated quality among pros is high level playing ability. Some of the worst pros I've known were top tier players. Passion for the game, caring deeply about all their students and the success of the program is what's

117

important. Unfortunately, there seems to be far too many pros today (especially among the young ones) that lack the essential communication skills to be successful. Being professional in all endeavors and striving to improve teaching and administrative skills is what ensures a pro's long-term success!"

Brad Holcombe

Chicago, Illinois

"A good pro will listen to his members and put programs in place that will help them develop their full potential in a fun and encouraging environment. They must be open-minded enough to modify their teaching habits to fit current trends, while keeping fundamentals and the integrity of the game in place."

Allison Ogden

Country Club of Salisbury
Salisbury, NC

"I feel a great tennis coach/instructor needs passion for the game. Without that passion, the instruction won't be effective. Patience and encouragement with the students are priceless, and the ability to tweak a few things as opposed to changing the student's entire game is also what I look for."

Denise Kyger

Country Club of Salisbury
Salisbury, NC

"An exceptional tennis professional must be passionate about the game of tennis and that passion should be obvious to every person he/she encounters in their workday environment. Excellent teaching professionals should inspire confidence in clients and give instruction for basic to advanced students with the same level of preparation and enthusiasm. Competent professionals should know their particular environment and be willing to adjust to expectations."

Brenda Culbertson

General Manager
Old Providence Racquet Club
Charlotte, NC

"Having been involved in competitive tennis for over 40 years, I've seen good pros and lots of bad pros. The really excellent ones all had the following traits in common:
- An intense passion for the game.
- A genuine interest in helping all their members improve.

- They watched their junior and adult members play – offering technical and tactical advice (without expecting pay). They did this because they wanted to!
- They got to know the members as people, their families and their children.
- They all had an exceptional work ethic, and they did whatever was necessary to make their programs succeed.
- They each were able to adapt their teaching methodology to the type of student being taught and get the most out of them.
- They all had great human relation skills, empathy and patience.

Finally, all the really good pros involved themselves in continuing education."

Jon Post

Former Tennis Committee member,
Country Club of Salisbury
Salisbury, NC

"What qualities does an excellent pro possess? First and foremost, they must genuinely care about their members –care for them as people. They have to know the families, the kids, be able to relate to them and should keep up with them over the years. This caring should extend to all facets of a pros work. A good pro never takes anything personally. For instance, if a member decides to take lessons from a pro at another club… a good pro embraces that! He/she should never take the position that "I'll never take them back as a student again!" We have over 230 ladies participating in interclub league play. Not all of them take lessons from us, but I care about all of them! I'm just excited by the fact that all of them want to play tennis!

I've found out through the years that a great deal can be learned from other successful pros. Indeed, a lot of my growth as a teaching professional has come this way. When I think back on the bad pros I've known, they all exhibited common traits. These included: a know-it-all attitude; lack of good human relation skills; an unwillingness to get along with other staff members; and a failure to get to know the members. Many of them also seemed more interested in landing their next big job rather than with doing a good job in their present position."

John Meyer

Director of Tennis
Olde Providence Racquet Club
Charlotte, NC

"The really good teaching professionals I've known all had similar traits. These included: extremely good human relation skills, a flexible teaching style – i.e., the ability to adapt their teaching style in accordance with the age/skill of their student(s), and patience. In addition, the good pros all had a thick hide – they didn't take criticism personally and they each – in their own way – had good diagnostic skills and were good listeners. My views come from the perspective of only having taught at country clubs. I've been the director of tennis at Carmel Country Club for five years now and I've been fortunate to have had good assistant pros. When I hire, I don't want another "me" – or in other words – a pro with my same teaching style/skills. I want our pros to have different teaching styles and personalities. I don't try to fix what weaknesses they have – but rather try to put them in a position where they can best employ their strengths. I've found that this approach results in a better tennis program. The bad pros I've seen also had similar traits. Most were lazy, lacked good human relation skills, didn't seem to care and weren't punctual. Many seemed to view members as dollar signs rather than human beings with feelings and needs. Some also had know-it-all attitudes and many failed to get along with the other tennis staff."

Katie Carpenter

Director of Tennis
Carmel Country Club
Charlotte, NC

Chapter 19

"Whatever you are – be a good one!"

Abraham Lincoln

**"Most of us who aspire to be tops in our fields don't really consider
the amount of work required to stay tops."**

Althea Gibson

**"Great teaching professionals strive to improve the quality of life in
the people at their club, camp or park. They play an admirable role as
a coach, role model, leader, or mentor. They understand that what
they do matters and makes a difference in helping the people around
them to be the best they can be."**

Kirk Anderson

PTR & USPTA Master Professional
Director of Coaching Education,
United States Tennis Association

Chapter 19: Conclusions/Final Thoughts

Writing this book was fun but extremely challenging. The subject matter was far different than that of my previous books co-authored with Gray Cook. From start to finish, this project took me about six- and one-half years. Like anything written, I'm sure I'll see subjects I could have/should have included, but I'll leave that up to you, the reader, to research.

The main points I hope you get from this book are as follows: the four most important ingredients for success in your career are 1) a strong work ethic, 2) good human relation skills, 3) good character, honesty, integrity and 4) excellent organizational and teaching skills. Knowing a lot about technology is great, but without these 4 attributes, you cannot succeed.

Keep an open mind in your learning but beware of so called "experts" who may be selling educational "snake oil". There are, and always have been, lots of these people in tennis. Be pragmatic in your approach and commit to being a lifelong learner.

 Much of what you have read is common sense, a quality that many in the tennis profession seem to ignore. If you have gained nothing else, understand that **you must be professional in all aspects of your work**. You exist for your clients, without them, you would have no job.

The measure of your success is very simple: a) do you have a good reputation? b) have your students gotten better as a result of your coaching? When I say better, I am referring to you helping them to become better tennis players as well as helping them become good citizens. The most successful teaching professionals are those that can work with what comprises 98.5% of the playing public – the 2.5 to 4.5 players – and make them better! Juniors and women are where the overwhelming lesson business is these days.

As you have read, there are many aspects of being a tennis professional that are rewarding. There are also many things that make the job very difficult. I know of no successful pro who hasn't, at one time or another, had to struggle to keep their job. It's just the nature of the business.

I'm now approaching my fifth decade of teaching tennis. I feel very fortunate to be employed in a profession that I love. I wake up every morning and am excited about the challenges facing me. Over the past forty-eight years, I have learned a great deal, but there is much I don't know, and I still relish the opportunity to learn. I still love to play and compete, but the greatest joy I get is in seeing my students improve. God willing, I'll be able to continue teaching for another ten to twelve years.

My career hasn't always been "easy sailing". I've experienced some rough times and, like anyone, have made some bad decisions. I have, however, learned from these situations and have grown as a result. This I know: If you're honest, treat everyone the same and always try your best, you'll survive these episodes. Indeed, you'll prosper today and in the future!

I am sure you have developed and implemented ideas that have made you a good pro. The "melding" of your ideas with what other great pros have done is the surest way of improving your teaching, administrative and human relation skills. Take pride in the fact that you're doing what only about 38,000 others (1 in 200,000 people) on the planet can do!

The road you'll travel will be rough at times, but if you love the game and helping others – in the end it'll be worth it. I wish you the best in all your future tennis endeavors!

Jack Thompson

About the Author

Jack Thompson

In a career that has spanned 48 years, Jack Thompson has been involved in virtually every aspect of tennis coaching, teaching, consulting, and programming. His experience includes 26 years as a Director of Tennis at clubs in Virginia and North Carolina, 8 years as a tennis academy Director and co-owner, and 6 years as the Head Men's and Women's tennis coach at Catawba College in Salisbury, North Carolina. From 1998 to 2004, Thompson's Catawba College teams compiled win records of 68% and his men's squad won the SAC conference in 2004, the first team to do so since 1946! Jack has produced 17 Virginia junior state champions and 14 North Carolina Junior State Champions. He also served as professional coach for his sister Leigh Thompson (WTA highest ranking # 27) in 1983 and 84. His partnership with colleague Gray Cook (arguably today's preeminent Sports and Orthopedic Physical Therapist) has produced 2 co-authored works: Power, Speed and Stamina for Tennis (1999) and Functional Tennis Training (Release Date Winter 2023). A Virginia Tech graduate, Jack has been a top 5-8 ranked player in singles and doubles in Virginia and North Carolina since 1988. In 2001, Jack was inducted as a PTR International Master Professional, 1 of only 41 among the PTR's worldwide membership of 16,000 certified members. Then, in 2015, Jack was honored as the Professional Tennis Registry (PTR) pro of the year at the PTR International Tennis Symposium in Hilton Head, SC. He has also authored numerous scholarly articles in the PTR's quarterly journal, TennisPro. He currently serves as the Director of Tennis for the city of Salisbury, North Carolina. In addition, he is also the Boys' Varsity Tennis Coach at the Gray Stone Day School in Misenheimer, MC and co-Director of Nike Tennis camps in Charlotte, NC. He resides with his wife of 45 years, Pamela, who is a professor of business at Catawba College and the University of North Carolina at Charlotte.

References

1. Richey, Cliff, Kallendorf, Hibire. (2009) <u>Acing Depression: A Tennis Champion's Toughest Match</u>. New Chapter Press (www.Newchaptermedia.com).

2. Tilden, Bill (1929) <u>Match Play and the Spin of the Ball</u>. Reissued 1969 by Kennikat Press, Port Washington N.Y.

3. Plagenhoef, Stanley (1970). <u>Fundamental of Tennis</u>. Prentice Hall Inc., Englewood Cliffs, N.J.

4. Talbert, Bill and Old, Bruce (1962). <u>The Game of Singles in Tennis</u>. J. B. Lippincott Co., Philadelphia and New York.

5. Talbert, Bill and Old, Bruce (1968). The Game of Doubles in Tennis. J. B. Lippincott Co., Philadelphia and New York.

6. Fox, Allen (1979). <u>If I'm the Better Player Why Can't I Win?</u> Published by: Nike Tennis Camps c/o U.S. Sports Development, 919 Sir Francis Drake Blvd, Kentfield, CA 94904.

7. Fox, Allen (1985). <u>Think to Win: The Strategic Dimension of Tennis</u>. Harper Collins Publishers, Inc., 10 East 53rd Street, New York, NY 10022.

8. Fox, Allen (2010). <u>Tennis: Winning the Mental Match</u>.

9. Roetert, Paul and Groppel, Jack (editors) (2001) <u>World Class Tennis Technique</u>. Human Kinetics Publishers Inc. P.O. Box 5076, Champaign, IL 61825-5076.

10. Saviano, Nick. (2002). <u>Maximum Tennis: 10 Keys to Unleashing your On-Court Potential</u>. Human Kinetics, Publishers Inc., P.O. Box 5076, Champaign, IL 61825-5076.

11. Cook, Gray and Thompson, Jack. (1999). <u>Power, Speed and Stamina for Tennis: A Complete Guide for the Player and Coach</u>. Kendall/Hunt Publishing Co. 4050 Westmark Dr., Dubuque, Iowa 52002.

12. Cook, Gray. (2003). <u>Athletic Body in Balance</u>. Human Kinetics Publishers Inc., P.O. Box 5076, Champaign, IL, 61825-5076.

13. Cook, Gray and Thompson, Jack. (2016). Functional <u>Tennis</u>. Thompsontennis.net; www.functionalmovmentsystems.com

14. Staniford, David and Boaz, Joan. (2010). Natural <u>Tennis, second edition</u>. Stipes Publishing L.L.C., 204 W. University Ave., Chicago, Ill., 61820

15. Pluim, Babette and Safran, Marc. (2004). From Breakpoint to Advantage. Racquet Tech Publishing (USRSA), 330 Main St., Vista, CA 92084.

16. <u>USPTA World Conference Q & A with Hall of Fame Inductee Peter Burwash.</u> Tennis Industry Magazine, Aug. 2016/Vol 44/No 8/pg. 48.

ID 119190923 © Chernetskaya, Dreamstime.com
Pg. 117 Opinions Wanted, Businessman working on holographic interface, Motion
    Graphics
    ID 99392659 © Stockbakery, Dreamstime.com
Pg. 129 Fork in the road surrounded with lush trees and grass
    ID 190701918 © Wirestock, Dreamstime.com
Pg. 131 *Author Photo*
    ID 20210913171934 ©Pam Thompson

Appendix I

Overly Involved Tennis Parents

As published in Tennis Pro Magazine

November/December 2014

(Reformatted to Fit this Publication)

Overly Involved Tennis Parents

More
Common
Today
than in
the Past

by Jack Thompson

A PTR International Master Professional, Jack has a graduate background in Exercise Physiology and Motor Learning. During his 33-year career, he has worked as a Head Professional and was Head Men's and Women's Tennis Coach at Catawba College in Salisbury, North Carolina. Jack is co-author of Power, Speed and Stamina for Tennis: A Complete Guide for the Player and Coach. An expanded second edition of the book he co-wrote with sport and orthopedic physical therapist, Gray Cook, is now available. A speaker at numerous PTR symposia, Jack is Head Pro and Co-Director of the Performance Tennis Academy at the Sportscenter in Concord, North Carolina.

Tennis parents. These two words conjure images of intrusive - sometimes abusive - parents living vicariously through their children's tennis. In all likelihood, they've been around since the game first came to the United States in the late 1880s. While the majority are good sports parents, a vocal minority have given tennis - and other sports - a bad name. This article explores this phenomenon and examines ways to deal with difficult parents.

Kids are kids. It's the parents who have changed over the past 30 years. It is painful to admit, but many in my generation have done a poor job of teaching their children responsibility, integrity, good character, self-reliance, work ethic, independence, resilience, and respect for peers and authority. These qualities are the quintessential building blocks for excellence in sport and, indeed, in life. The children of my generation are now parents themselves and their kids are playing tennis. Our children, and now our grandchildren, lack important values and it's our fault.

These observations are supported by a majority of schoolteachers, tennis pros, coaches, administrators, lawyers, law enforcement officers and counselors. Any seasoned coach or schoolteacher will tell you that it's common today for parents to question their methods (teaching, disciplinary). When children fail, it is often regarded as their teachers' fault, and if parents don't get their way, they immediately take their complaint to the principal. If that doesn't work, they go to whomever is higher in command. Good teachers and coaches try to develop students' character, honesty, self-reliance, respect for peers and authority, and how to recover from failure, but many parents want no part of it.

PTR Professional, Marvin Hedgepeth, a career public school teacher and tennis coach with more than 35 years' experience, told me,

Some years ago, at the start of tryouts for the spring tennis season, one of my returning starters missed five of the first seven days of practice, because he had a part-time job at a grocery store. I made it clear that even last year's starters had to attend daily practices. When I posted the final team roster for the upcoming season, his name was not included. Sure enough, the next day his mother delivered a seething letter to my principal, demanding that I be fired as tennis coach. After being assured that attending practices was mandatory, my principal supported my decision, much to the dismay of the angry mother.

Obviously, this mother didn't understand personal responsibility. Would she think her son could have kept his job at the grocery store if he failed to show up for five consecutive days? Of course not!

Colin Rudisill, a fellow tennis professional who has been teaching for 28 years, shared his experience.

Over the last five years, I estimate that more than 50% of my time has involved coaching parents - not kids. I'm talking about teaching parents how to be supportive, but not intrusive, in their children's tennis. Parents today are definitely problematic in this regard!

It seems there has been a paradigm shift in the mind set of parents. It has gone from teaching their children to learn how to lose gracefully before learning how to win, to today's belief that there is only winning. Also, if their child loses, it's not their fault, it's time to change coaches. No longer are our kids being parented to strive for excellence through hard work, to never give up, and to be receptive to the guidance of their coaches and teachers. Those values have been replaced by a strong sense of entitlement, i.e., that kids have the right to question authority and they have a right to exhibit bad behaviors with no consequences.

It certainly didn't used to be that way. The kids of yesteryear rarely stepped out of line, but when they did, their parents took charge. In his book *Levels of the Game*, John McPhee recounts an incident in 1953, involving a 10-year-old named Arthur Ashe. Arthur had been accepted for inclusion in a year-round training group run by Dr. Walter Johnson at his home in Lynchburg, Virginia (he had a court in his backyard). Soon after he arrived, Arthur began questioning Dr. Johnson's methods. Specifically, he implied that his previous coach, Ron Charity, knew more than Johnson. Dr. Johnson called Arthur's father, and suggested he pick up his son, as he felt the youngster was uncoachable. McPhee wrote,

Having grown up during the 1960s (I was born in 1953) and now having coached in three different decades, I can say that too many parents have changed - and not for the better. I ran cross country and track in high school - from the 8th to the 12th grade - successfully competing at the state and national levels. My teammates and I would never have thought about questioning a coach's knowledge or directions. Likewise, our parents would never (and didn't) intervene on our behalf. The teachers, administrators and coaches were right and that was that! Our parents didn't permit us to whine and make excuses. They taught us that we must take personal responsibility for our actions.

In a *Washington Post* article, Kathleen Parker wrote,

Illustrating Parker's observations is the experience of a respected coach, we'll call John, who ran several successful tennis academies. A 14-year-old had been taking private lessons with John. After one of the lessons, her mother said, "My daughter doesn't like it when you hit your backhand to her with slice." Being both patient and courteous, John replied, "It's very important that she learn how to return a ball with that kind of spin…and we're working on that. She'll definitely encounter slices in competitive play." The mother responded," Well, I'd like her to hit against topspin." To that, John continued, a little less patiently," I'll see to it she hits against balls she'll encounter in match play." I wonder if this mother would have been so bold as to complain if her child were hitting with Grand Slam Champions Steffi Graf or Ken Rosewall, both of whom hit backhands only with slice and are considered to have the best slice backhands ever.

Another time, John and student were engaged in a strategic lesson. This type of lesson, of course, requires more talking than would be involved in a drilling or shot repetition lesson. Considering that her strokes were good, but that she didn't understand the first thing about constructing points, this type of lesson was exactly what the young lady needed. When she played school and USTA events, she had the same outcome each time; she beat players she should beat (those with weaker strokes who couldn't construct points) and lost to players she could have beaten (players with the same strokes and a little better knowledge of singles tactics). John had explained to both the student and her mother that a 'see ball, hit ball' strategy could only take her so far. This advice was partially understood by the student, but not at all by her mother.

At the completion of the strategy lesson, the mother approached John and said, "My daughter is in track, basketball and cheerleading, [can you see the overbooked schedule here?] and every second of her time on the court should involve ball hitting. You talked too much during that lesson." John explained that talking was necessary in a strategic lesson in order for her daughter to grasp the concepts. He explained his credentials and said, "Your daughter needs to learn how to play the game - she already knows how to hit the ball. If you doubt my coaching, perhaps you should seek another coach - one who's all about just hitting balls." She replied, "Oh, I'm not doubting your resume. It's just that I think she needs to always be hitting the ball." As you can see, Mom just didn't get it, didn't want to get it, and refused to listen.

One might wonder if this tennis mother treats her family physician the same way. Can you imagine a doctor telling her that she has a swollen spleen and her responding, "No, you need to treat me for diabetes"? As it turned out, the relationship between John and student ended, and she began taking lessons from an instructor who feeds balls 90% of the lesson. Predictably, she is no more advanced as a player today than she was when she stopped working with John. This kind of intrusion from a parent was unheard of in the 1960s, 70s, 80s, and even early 90s. During those decades, if children had complained about any aspect of the coaching they received, their parents would have told them to listen to their coach and to do as he says, because he's the expert! Many of my colleagues have had similar experiences with parents.

There is no doubt that this kind of parental behavior has become much more common, and it certainly isn't limited to the sport of tennis. Bill King, a successful football coach with 30 years of experience on the field and in the classroom shared the following,

Kids over the past 30 years are in many ways the same. It's the parents who have changed - they've stopped being parents! A glowing example of this comes from my last season of coaching. The parents wanted us to impose a curfew on our players - something that we obviously couldn't enforce. How in the world could my staff enforce a curfew at their homes? That's the job of the parents! The other thing that changed is the sense of entitlement from both the kids and the parents - even the guys on the second team felt entitled to a scholarship!

Rena Goolsby, a tennis professional with more than 28 years' experience coaching both juniors and adults puts it this way,

When I first came to tennis as a player and later as an instructor, the parents' attitudes were to let the coach, coach. I see parents today come to the court with a sense of entitlement that their child should win. You can't lay all the blame, however, at the parents' feet. Our culture has changed to the point that parents are told if their child is not enrolled in a certain preschool, their college career is over. This attitude, of course, bleeds over to the tennis court.

In my conversations with college tennis coaches across the country, an alarming number offer to explain why they recruit foreign players. Many feel that US players are much more likely to whine, complain, and be more difficult to coach. Moreover, the sentiment is that foreign parents rarely, if ever, intervene in the coaching process. Personally, I feel that this is a cop out. Coaches should seek to fill their rosters with US players in order to improve tennis in the states; however, I understand why these coaches feel as they do.

These beliefs and behaviors are not only more commonplace today in sport, but in academia as well. Adair Doran, who has 30 years' experience in the classroom teaching advanced placement (AP) European History, AP US Government and Politics, and AP Psychology, contends,

Parents today question grades, they question homework. Many assume that if their child just comes to class, they'll automatically make an A. When I first entered the profession, this was not the case!

Another public-school teacher, Karla Williams, with 34 years' experience relates,

More and more I see parents with the mindset that their child can do no wrong. If a child makes a mistake, parents bail them out by making excuses for them. They expect other children to be of high character, but there is no accountability for their child. Problems are blamed on something other than the child's behavior. Teachers are blamed for students' bad behavior. One example involved an elementary school age child who was causing serious problems in the classroom. The parent had meetings with the teacher, principal, counselor, and school psychologist. After one such meeting, the parent was overheard asking the child, "What did your teacher do to make you do that?"

In our schools, principals seem to have their hands tied by pressures from complaining parents. Teachers are afraid to address discipline problems, and many real issues are swept under the carpet. If teachers ask for help in their class, they are perceived as weak teachers, not able to engage their students. Students know when they are in control, and lack of respect for those in authority continues to escalate.

Parents often do projects or assignments for their child. In the classroom, we see students not completing assignments, as they expect others to do the work for them, or they rush just to 'get it done' without putting in time or effort. We also see children who give up or are not willing to try anything new for fear they will not be good enough to meet their parent's approval. Even as children, they feel tremendous pressure to be perfect.

I wish parents understood that it is much more enjoyable and easier to give glowing reports about a child, but when someone truly cares, they will point out things that need changing. If parents would be willing to listen to early warnings, they would be helping their child learn life lessons that could prevent them from making bigger mistakes later on..

Far too many parents today feel entitled to tell teachers how to teach and coaches how to coach. If their child breaks rules (e.g., doesn't follow directions, talks when the teacher is talking, or demonstrates poor sportsmanship) and the coach has to invoke discipline, it is all too common to receive an angry email or phone call from the parents. It is as if the pro has implied that the behavior is the parents' fault, and they want you to know their child is a good kid!

My parents demanded that I follow the rules laid down by my coaches and teachers. I was a good kid, but at times I did break the rules, and when I did, I was punished first at school and again when I got home. Regrettably, I'm not seeing many parents today teaching their children to take personal responsibility for their actions, and the results have been catastrophic. In my opinion and that of many of my colleagues, kids are nowhere near as tough as their 1960s, 70s and 80s counterparts. Con- fronted with failure, too many are coddled and told that the situation is unfair. If they don't make the team, the parent shoves them into another sport. If they fail at that one, they keep trying to find them one in which they can succeed without having to work very hard, or the kid drops sports altogether.

Too many sports programs don't keep score and give trophies to all the kids. Failure is now viewed as damaging to children's emotional health!

In the parents' relentless pursuit of success for their children, they actually weaken their character and make them less resilient to failure and far less likely to overcome adversity. In the final analysis, isn't that what ten-nis is all about? Every single point is really nothing more than overcoming adversity. Indeed, life itself is a series of opportunities to overcome adversity. With good parenting, children can learn to embrace challenges, eventually learning that failure isn't fatal. They learn how to get back up, dust themselves off, and work harder next time toward achieving that goal.

This trend has weakened our country in sports, as well as in society. In US tennis, the decline is obvious. In 1981, the US had 39 men and 51 women ranked in the top 100, today we have 5 men and 10 women ranked in the top 100 in singles. Rugged individualism and personal enterprise have given way to the notion that if you fail, it's not your fault and some- one will bail you out, whether it's deserved or not. We're neither respect- ed by our allies nor feared by our enemies, and that certainly pertains to our tennis. Almost any Davis Cup squad now feels they have a good chance against the United States team, and they are right!

I hope parents who read this recognize themselves and will wake up and make changes. It is my hope that they will understand that the role of good tennis parents is to pay for the lessons, allow the coach to do his/her job, support their children emotionally, mete out discipline when they behave badly on the court, and when they fail, encourage them to 'stick it out' and do the hard work necessary to improve.

As the great basketball coach John Wooden once said,

Failure is not fatal. Failure to change might be.

He also offered valuable advice that could apply to parents who attempt to tell coaches how to coach,

All the important things you'll ever learn in life come after you know it all!

How true.

What can you do about it?

Schedule a meeting with the parent *before* any coaching begins. Whether you're a country club professional, private/public club teaching pro or high school tennis coach, it is imperative that you clearly define your role and rules to parents. I have found that this is best achieved in a parents meeting (group meeting for academy/school/clinic students and, an individual meeting for students taking private lessons). Position the conversation to get them on your side. Strategize so you are working together as a team for the good of their child. Discuss their expectations, as well as your own.

During this meeting you should explain,

- that considerable time will be devoted to developing strong character, good sportsmanship, independence, self-reliance, integrity, taking responsibility for one's actions, and respect for peers and coaches.

- that students will be taught that failure is a part of personal growth and how they can embrace the challenge of working harder following failure.

- that you will not attempt to parent the child and that parents shouldn't attempt to coach.

- that if you must discipline their child, the parent needs to support you.

- that everyone doesn't get a trophy in your program. As in life, only exceptional achievement will be rewarded (e.g., only the champion and finalist receive awards in your tournaments/leagues).

Have a written list of your rules and expectations with a place for the pro, child, and parent(s) to sign (with the pro retaining one copy and the parent receiving the other) is a great idea. In the event that a child or parent is not adhering to policy, then you have solid documentation for action. Finally, if a parent or child continually poses problems, you MUST terminate the relationship. Doing so may lose you a little business initially, but in the long term you'll end up having more 'coachable' and successful players.

References

1. McPhee, John. "Levels of the Game." (1969) Farrar, Straus and Giroux, NY. pp 41-42.

2. Parker, Kathleen. "What Steve Jobs Can Teach Us About Failure." October 16, 2011. The Salisbury Post (reprinted from the Washington Post). Page 6D

Appendix II

10 Most Common Mistakes
Made by Tennis Professionals

As published in Tennis Pro Magazine

May/June 2014

(Reformatted to Fit this Publication

10 Most Common Mistakes

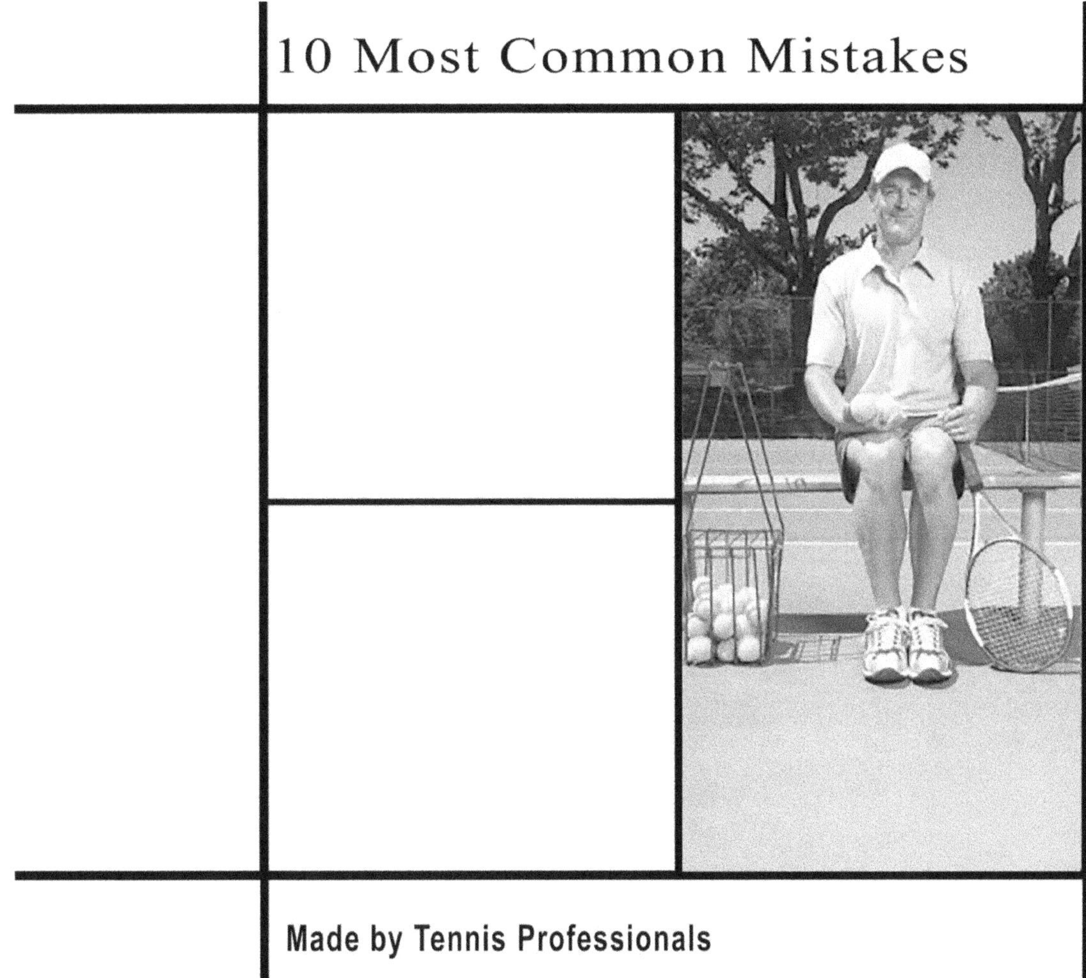

Made by Tennis Professionals

by Jack Thompson

A PTR International Master Professional, Jack has a graduate back- ground in Exercise Physiology and Motor Learning. During his 33-year career, he has worked as a Head Professional and was Head Men's and Women's Tennis Coach at Catawba College in Salisbury, North Carolina. Jack is co-author of Power, Speed and Stamina for Tennis: A Complete Guide for the Player and Coach. An expanded second edition of the book he co-wrote with sport and orthopedic physical therapist, Gray Cook, is now available. A speaker at numerous PTR symposia, Jack is Head Pro and Co-Director of the Performance Ten- nis Academy at the Sportscenter in Concord, North Carolina.

Teaching tennis can be an immensely rewarding experience. Helping people attain their goals and giving them a sport that improves their quality of life has kept me in the profession for 33 years. Good teaching is both an art and a science. Indeed, the best coaches become students of the game, and their development is the result of many years of experience in a number of areas. This includes certification, learning from other seasoned professionals, teaching experience and creativity, reading the really good books - past and present, an ongoing quest for professional development, which includes course work and attending tennis symposia, playing experience, tournament administration, community service, service to your professional organization, pro-grammatic development and other tennis related activities. Without question, today's tennis professional must wear many hats, but a large part of what we do today still involves instruction.

The purpose of this article is to identify the 10 most common teaching mistakes pros make. More importantly, suggestions are offered on how to avoid these pitfalls and improve your teaching. Keep in mind that any such list is purely opinion - there are other mistakes to avoid.

1. Failure to Teach Character, Self-Reliance and Independence

I hate to say it, but teaching character, self-reliance and independence is a rarity these days. Pros are under such pressure from all sides to get kids playing as quickly as possible that, in most programs, these virtues are not being taught. Dr. Allen Fox wrote an excellent article on this topic entitled *Producing the Next Great Champion*. You can read it online at:

www.allenfoxtennis.net/?p=34

Teaching these should be priority number one, and it should be an ongoing process. Players need to understand what it means to be a fair and ethical competitor. Students should learn respect for adults and respect their opponents. They should be taught to figure out how to win on their own. They need to understand that making excuses for losses or subpar play is not good sportsmanship, and that there's a right way and wrong way to handle cheating. Pros should teach their students that cheating, in any form, is reprehensible and is the hallmark of weak character. The coach needs to place a premium on integrity - doing what you say you're going to do when you say you'll do it.

Not too long ago, an acquaintance told me a disturbing story that illustrates what's going on in some (hopefully few) programs. She took her son, who had done well in their USTA section, to the academy of a very high-profile coach. She asked the coach to take a look at her child and to do an assessment on how good he might be with intensive training. As the coach and the parent passed by one of the courts a 10-year-old player made a very bad call during a practice match. Both the coach and parent saw it. The coach said, "You know, when a kid is 10, I don't mind so much if they occasionally cheat. It shows they really have a desire to win, and I let the kids know that." The parent was stunned and enrolled her child in another academy.

The point is that we're getting away from teaching the big picture. Winning is the ultimate goal, but not at the expense of being fair, respectful and demonstrating good character. I think a lot of pros today are some- what afraid to harp on these things for fear they'll lose a student to the guy up the road who's all about just hitting balls. I believe strongly that the pros who focus on character development, as well as tennis, set themselves ahead of the competition and, in the long run, end up with much more business.

2. Over Teaching

This is an area where entry level pros are vulnerable. It's so easy (I know, I certainly did it) for a young teacher to overload their students with too much information. Doing this emanates from the desire to do a good job, so every bit of minutia is described in great detail. The teacher talks incessantly, even during hitting, micromanaging every aspect of the student's stroke. What typically happens in these instances is that the student becomes too teacher dependent. Students stop trying to figure out how to adapt their strokes/tactics in order to succeed in match play.

Like writing a good paper, a good teacher should seek to impart the most concise and meaningful information to students of all levels. Some pros are addicted to hearing themselves talk! It's true that more information must be covered with beginning students, however, even in these instances, the teacher must strive to stick to the essential points and avoid excessive communication.

3. Too Much Dead Ball Work

I've written an entire article on this point (*TennisPro* November/December 2013). Without restating everything I wrote in that piece, suffice it to say that I feel there's far too much dead ball work being used by tennis teachers today, particularly in the United States.

Certainly, there's value in this form of training, especially with beginning students and players who are working their way back into the game following an injury or surgery. Additionally, it's an excellent way to help players whose strokes are in a slump. Basket feeding is also useful when working with students who are changing grips or learning a new shot. My problem with dead ball work is in seeing teachers using it excessively with students who have decent strokes. What's excessive? The question itself is a bit problematic, but I'd say that if more than 20% of training time (with students who have acceptable strokes) is dead ball in nature - then that's too much!

Basket feeding drills don't force students to adjust to the various spins, speeds and depths of shots encountered in match play. Moreover, there is no pressure to win (or lose) a point. Basket fed students never perform well in match play compared to their live ball trained counterparts. The principle of specificity of training in the field of motor learning predicts this. Once players develop sound strokes, then the majority of their training time should be devoted to live ball work, learning tactics and strategy, and playing practice matches.

If lots of dead ball work were the answer to player development, then over the past 20 years we would have seen large numbers of Americans ranked in the top 100 internationally. Regrettably, the reverse has been the case and the drop has been dramatic! In fact, it has almost been a complete inverse relationship. The greater the frequency of dead ball work, the fewer the number of really good match players. Obviously, there are other reasons we're failing in this endeavor, but too much dead ball work has certainly contributed!

4. Teaching Only One Way to Hit Groundstrokes

This one really gets me. If there's one thing that we, as teachers of tennis, should have learned is that there is no 'gold standard' as to how ground- strokes are hit. There are many different methods that fall within the para- meters of what's correct. Look at the forehand drives of Rafael Nadal, Roger Federer, Pete Sampras and Rod Laver. Each has very different backswings and grips, but the thing they all have in common is sound fundamentals!

Purveyors of the only-a-semi-western-or-western-grip-with-a-circular-backswing-forehand philosophy fail to realize what's most important. If a player has good ball control, can hit consistently with varying spins (which can be used for control, defense or offense), can hit with disguise and power when needed, then the stroke is sound.

Not too long ago a friend of mine applied for an assistant job with a well-known director of tennis. He asked my friend, "So what's your philosophy on teaching a forehand drive?" My friend replied in a manner similar to what I stated above. The DOT said, "Well, I require all my assistants to teach our students to use a western or semi-western grip. I want them to teach all open stances from the baseline. Now, are you going to do this?" My friend responded by asking, "What if a kid can hit a killer forehand, but uses an eastern grip?" To this the DOT responded, "That's not the way it's done today. I'd want you to change it!"

Unbelievable! Needless to say, my friend wasn't offered the job - nor did he want it. Unfortunately, far too many pros think this way!

5. Focusing All Efforts on Working with Only the 'Best' Players

This is among the top reasons pros get fired. Many pros throw out a loaf of bread to the best players and crumbs to the lesser skilled students whose parents pay most of the bills! This mistake has its roots in the pro's misguided belief that developing top ranked juniors will bring them admiration, fame and fortune. In reality, the reverse is true. The vast majority of the instructional business and programmatic activity at most clubs is at the 3.0-3.5 level of play. The women are the lesson and clinic takers. Juniors, too, are quite important, but again, emphasis should be placed on building players who have little or no skills. Twenty years ago, a pro may have been able to get away with being a one trick pony, but not today!

6. Failure to Teach Tactics/Strategy to Each Developmental Level of Student

At every level of play, the pro should be teaching percent- age tactics and strategy. At the beginning level, the majority of instructional time should be devoted to stroke mechanics. For some time, the sole tactical objective should be to *keep the ball in play at all cost* - anywhere within the court boundaries. As a student improves and they learn directional control, they can be coached to hit most shots to their opponent's weakness. Once the student has mastered depth control and spin, more advanced strategy (serve and volley, drop shots, etc.) can be taught.

Regrettably, many pros ignore teaching strategy, assuming the students will pick it up on their own. In the majority of cases, students are unable to do so.

7. Failure to Teach Slices, Volleying and Mid-Court Skills Early in a Junior's Development

This one is closely related to the preceding point. Without a well-rounded game, a student is severely limited as to how s/he can win. Take, for instance, a junior player who only has a topspin forehand drive and topspin backhand drive. If his/her opponent is 10-15% better at it than s/he is, the outcome is certain - a loss. With slices and volleying skills, the junior (if losing at trading ground- strokes) would be able to draw the opponent to the net or would be able to come in him/herself.

I believe strongly that students should be taught very early how to slice, how to half volley, volley and hit overheads. I further believe that by age 12, they should have all the shots – top spins, slice, flat shots. They may not be able to use every one of them effectively in match play, but if fed a ball, they would be able to demonstrate all shots. In my opinion, far too many juniors today are unable to slice well, return a good slice that is hit to them, and volley proficiently. As a result, many juniors today look like 4.5-5.0 players from the baseline and morph into a 3.5 when approaching the net!

8. Failure to Summarize at the End of a Lesson & Failure to Tell the Student How and How Much to Practice

This seems to be very commonplace. Any good lesson, whether it be a music lesson or sports related lesson, should end with a short summary period high- lighting the most important points. Furthermore, the pro should clearly spell out how and how frequently the player(s) should practice.

9. Failure to Attend Seminars, Lectures & Workshops for Professional Development

This is an absolute must! If you want to be the best, you have to learn from the best, or as one of my mentors once said, "You learn from the best and create the rest!"

It is indeed naive (or arrogant) to believe you know it all. We learn from others and others learn from us. Knowledge comes from the sharing of ideas. I have always believed that the pursuit of coaching excellence is a journey - not a destination. Just like your tennis game - when you stop trying to improve - you stop being good!

Attending the annual PTR Tennis Symposium is extremely important and yet, on a percentage basis, very few tennis pros do.

This can be a time-consuming endeavor and may not yield direct income. Yet it is critical to develop students to their full potential. It's very important to see how students perform in the heat of battle - how they handle stress, and how they select and execute their shots. I have always made the time to go to matches and have found, in the overwhelming majority of cases, both the students and their parents appreciate it. Moreover, it puts you ahead of the pros who don't!

There are certainly other mistakes that a teaching professional can make. This article could have been turned into a book. Making mistakes is a natural part of growing in any profession. Try not to make any on this Top 10 list, and you'll be well on your way to a successful career in tennis!

Appendix III

Are American Coaches Using Too Many Dead Ball Drills?

As published in Tennis Pro Magazine

November/December 2013

(Reformatted to Fit this Publication)

Are American Coaches Using
Too Many Dead Ball Drills?

by Jack Thompson

A PTR International Master Professional, Jack has a graduate background in Exercise Physiology and Motor Learning. During his 33-year career, he has worked as a Head Professional and was Head Men's and Women's Tennis Coach at Catawba College in Salisbury, North Carolina. Jack is co-author of Power, Speed and Stamina for Tennis: A Complete guide for the Player and Coach. An expanded second edition of the book he co-wrote with sport and orthopedic physical therapist, Gray Cook, is now available. A speaker at several PTR symposia, Jack is Head Pro and Co-Director of the Performance Tennis Academy at the Sportscenter in Concord, North Carolina

Dead ball or feeding drills have been used by tennis coaches and teaching professionals for many years. In the early 80s, with the advent of tennis academies, their use burgeoned, and today, one would be hard pressed to see professionals not using some form of dead ball work.

These observations notwithstanding, several questions have arisen regarding dead ball drills. Is this the best way to train competitive players? What about 'live ball' work? Should both training methods be used? If not, when should the teacher cease using feeding drills?

The purpose of this article is to educate - not denigrate - a particular training philosophy and hopefully, improve today's tennis teaching. My opinion on this subject is based on sound scientific principles from the field of motor learning (the sports science discipline that examines how humans learn motor skills and the best methods of training those skills.

Let's begin with an overview of dead ball training. From this point forward, I'll be using the terms 'basket feeding drills' and 'dead ball drills' interchangeably, even though not all feeding drills are dead ball in nature. Technically any tennis drill that involves the teacher repetitively feeding (by hand or with a racquet) balls to students would be considered dead ball. The students hit one ball and then the teacher feeds another and so on. The feeds are almost always uniform in terms of speed, depth, spin and height of bounce. A great number of balls can be hit in a short period of time.

The benefits/advantages of this kind of training are:

1. It's an excellent, indeed the only way, to teach a beginner. Sound fundamentals can be developed for all the strokes with this approach.

2. It's the most effective means of teaching most players if changing a grip or if major changes have to be made in stroke mechanics.

3. It's an excellent way of teaching footwork.

4. It's a great way to enhance cardiovascular endurance. (Example: student runs for a drop shot, then runs for a lob, next runs for a drop shot, then runs for a lob, etc.)

5. It can be used effectively with advanced players whose strokes 'go off'.

6. It can be beneficial in working out players who are recovering from injury.

Is dead ball work then the best method to train all players? Are these types of drills being used too much today in America? The answer to these questions, in my opinion and the opinion of many of my peers, is no and yes respectively.

Let's take the first question and explore the reasons why dead ball drilling is not the best means of training all players.

In motor learning, there is a principle (principles are closely related to laws) known as specificity of training. This tenet, which has repeatedly been verified through research since the late 1950s, states that the training activities that have the greatest benefit on performance are those that simulate the mechanics, energy requirements, tactics and cognitive functioning required in competition.

It is applicable not only to tennis, but to all sports. This principle is not debatable. It is not personal opinion, and it is not derived from just anecdotal evidence. It is an accepted scientific premise derived from decades of hard data.

It should therefore, become obvious why dead ball drills should be used very sparingly with players whose strokes fall within accepted parameters of 'correctness'. Dead ball drills don't involve rallies. They don't replicate the random nature of spin, speed and height of bounce encountered in match play. Additionally, dead ball drills don't require critical thinking and there is no consequence to missing shots, as there is during match play. Furthermore, basket feeding can promote psychological dependency on the coach as s/he makes comments on each small adjustment the student must make. Hence, students often stop thinking for themselves.

Excessive use of dead ball drills would be analogous to:

1. A baseball batter only hitting perfectly thrown pitches at the same height, same speed and to same area within the strike zone.

2. A boxer only working out on the light or heavy bag or sparring against other boxers who throw the same punches in the same sequences every time.

3. A quarterback who only throws to a receiver with no defenders or handing off to a running back without the defensive linemen rushing.

4. A basketball player who only practices catching perfectly thrown passes, dribbling around cones, performing layups, etc., without opposing players pressuring him/her.

The list is endless, but certainly no other sport would train excessively using these techniques, and if they did, their competitive play would suffer considerably. Yet that's what's being done a lot today in tennis.

Support for the use of live ball work is widespread throughout the coaching community. The following is a sampling of what other experts have to say about the use of live ball vs. dead ball drilling.

> *The image that comes to mind when one thinks of tennis drills is an instructor constantly feeding balls to a line of people. This type of drill is called a dead ball drill.*
>
> *Although it's still used today, it is probably not the most effective way to prepare students for matches. Players only hit one or just a few balls on occasion, and they don't participate in a point.*
>
> *Individuals who practice dead ball drills constantly perform poorly in matches. It's mostly because the instructor feeds the balls perfectly to the students. Consistent feeds prevent players from adapting to different varieties of balls.*
>
> *The most effective, as well as most preferable, kinds of drills are live drills. Every tennis coach should attempt to make drills game-like and engaging.[7]*
>
> *-Tennis Spain*

Using too much dead ball work is why coaches hear their players complain, "I played horribly and just can't understand it.
In the lesson, I was hitting my forehand just fine." What happens is that players prepare for matches with way too much stroke repetition without creating a game like environment during practice sessions. Then, in the random environment of a real match, their strokes are challenged in a totally different way.
Players are simply not prepared. Their strokes naturally break down and they get frustrated and nervous. The more nervous they become, the more their strokes fall apart. It's a vicious cycle that is very difficult to break in the middle of a match.

Minimize dead ball drilling. Simulate real match performance in practice and your real match performance will improve automatically.[2]

- Joe Dinoffer, PTR International Master Professional

The disadvantage of a dead ball drill is that the drill does not simulate the back and forth hitting that happens when you are playing a point and thus, does not adequately prepare you for competition
It also inadvertently can diminish anticipation skills of reading cues from your opponent's strokes and positioning.
The advantage of a live ball drill over a dead ball drill is that a good live ball drill naturally simulates actual game situations with variations, such as different speeds, spins, location, height of bounce and so on.
These types of drills more closely simulate what happens in match play providing greater carry over from practice to play.[1]

- Nick Saviano, PTR International Master Professional

If all a coach does is basket feed, the motor pattern is acquired, but it will transfer little or not at all to real game play, because the skill is isolated and not set into a realistic tactical environment.
In other words, the player will know 'how' to stroke, but not getting repetition on why and when to use the skills, and this prevents students from using it successfully in match play. In motor learning there is a rule:
the transfer of learning between two situations is directly proportionate to the degree they are similar.
This is why many drills are good for exercise and general hitting but do little to transform the way people play. By recreating a realistic tennis situation [in a drill], *the skills learned will transfer to match play more effectively.[4]*

- Wayne Elderton, Head of Tennis Canada Coaching, Development and Certification in British Columbia

---

The more you can make practice drills appear like (simulate) the tactics needed in an actual match, the better the crossover value both technically and strategically.[5]

- Jose Higueras, USTA Director of Coaching for Player Development

---

The principle of specificity states that training is of the greatest benefit when it reflects the requirements of the actual performance.
Consequently, optimal competitive tennis performance would be achieved through a training program that is similar to the characteristics and demands of match play.[3]

- Dr. Sarah Morante, Director of Tennis Coaches Australia and contributing writer to Medicine and Science in Tennis

The important thing to remember in this discussion is dead ball drills should be used with students learning strokes. However, once they have acceptable strokes - and those strokes don't have to be perfect - the teacher should switch to predominately live ball work and match play. This is the only way students can learn how to adapt to the constantly changing conditions of match play. If problems do arise with stroke technique, the coach should immediately address the problem(s) and basket feeding may be necessary.

Good coaching is both an art and a science. The science has been presented in this article. The art is knowing when to wean players away from dead ball work. It is my firm opinion that today, too many coaches and pros, especially the younger ones, spend excessive amounts of training time with dead ball work. Far too many teachers continue using these drills long after they have served their purpose. I base this view on numerous visits to tennis academies in many states, conversations with hundreds of parents, players and pros, and reading what's being written in the print media.

So, what about the comment from some pros, "I used basket feeding drills with so-and-so, and look how well s/he did!" The point here is not how good the student did, but how much better they could have been if sound scientific principles had been used in their training! Like the old saying goes, "Practice like you play or you'll play like you practice!"

There is another problem - a closely related one that I'm seeing in the United States today. Our junior players do not play enough practice matches. I am very insistent that our students do this in our North Carolina tennis academy. I bombard them with emails on the subject and speak directly to the parents and players. I recommend that they play two practice matches per week, particularly during the 'off' months. Almost without exception, they do not follow this advice, so I know it's not being done in any of the other states. Conversations with other pros verify this observation. Incidentally, when I speak of a practice match, I do not count playing in a tournament. A practice match involves calling up another player, setting a time and site, and playing a best 2 out of 3 set match.

I am fully confident that if the majority of pros and coaches implement these suggestions, then we'll see American players - in large numbers - among the international elite.

Summary

1. Use dead ball drills when:
    - working with beginners
    - changing grips
    - teaching footwork
    - changing stroke mechanics
    - training for cardiovascular endurance
    - to warm up or cool down your players
    - a player's stroke(s) go into a slump
    - a player is recovering from injury/surgery

2. As soon as possible – with all students – integrate live ball hitting. Richard Schönborn said regarding basket feeding with beginners, "The ball is thus hit from the coach's hand and returned aimlessly by the player. There are no rallies, which normally is the stimulation, the aim and content of the game of tennis. As long as (which is very frequently in beginners), the ball is returned far away from the coach, it is acceptable, but if the ball is playable by the coach, he should hit it back directly. First of all, the player has more fun. Secondly, he learns to handle different situations more quickly, thirdly, he arns the rallying rhythm early on, and fourthly, he develops substantially greater perception and anticipation ability."[9]

3. The overwhelming amount of training time for tournament players should be spent on live ball work. After all, have you ever seen two college players, or two pros go out and do nothing but basket feed to each other? I don't think I've ever seen that with two good high school players! Live ball drilling with point values forces players to think their way through competitive situations and adjust their foot- work and shot selections to meet constantly changing conditions. It also aids the student in learning how to construct points. Players who are primarily ball fed never seem to be able to compete well, and the principle of specificity of training supports this observation.

4. Used in conjunction with predominately live ball work, basket feeding can be an asset. My recommendation is no more than 20% dead ball drilling with players who have sound strokes.

5. Tennis teachers need to stress - emphatically - to their students how important it is for them to play practice matches.

References

1) Saviano, Nick (2003). Maximum Tennis: 10 Keys to Unleashing Your On Court Potential. Human Kinetics Publishers, pgs 121-122.

2) Dinoffer, Joe (2003). Tennis Practice games. Human Kinetics Publishers, pg xi.

3) Morante, Sara (2006). Training Recommendations based on Match Characteristics of Professional Singles Tennis. Medicine and Science in Tennis, Volume 11, NR 3.

4) Elderton, Wayne (2002). To Drill or Not to Drill.

Coach to Coach. pg.1.

5) Higueras, Jose. Bringing Dead Ball Drills To Life. High Performance Coaching. Volume 10, No. 1.

6) Smith, David W. (2000). Coaching Mastery: The Ultimate Blueprint for Tennis Coaches, Tennis Parents, Tennis Teaching Professionals. Manahanken Printing, Canada. pg. 136.

7) What Are the Best Tennis Drills? (July 18, 2011). Tennis in Spain. pg 1.

8) Schönborn, Richard (2000). Advanced Techniques for Competitive Tennis (2nd ed.). Oxford: Meyer and Meyer Sport (UK)Ltd. pg 116.

Ibid, pg 114.

Appendix IV

A Better Model for Developing

Female Tennis Players

As published in Tennis Pro Magazine

July/August 2014

(Reformatted to Fit this Publication

A Better Model for Developing
Female Tennis Players

By Jack Thompson

A PTR International Master Professional, Jack has a graduate background in Exercise Physiology and Motor Learning. During his 34-year career, he has worked as a Head Professional and was Head Men's and Women's Tennis Coach at Catawba College in Salisbury, North Carolina. Jack is co-author of Power, Speed and Stamina for Tennis: A Complete Guide for the Player and Coach. An expanded second edition of the book he co-wrote with sport and orthopedic physical therapist, Gray Cook, is now available. A speaker at numerous PTR symposia, colleges and clubs, Jack is the Head Pro and co-Director of Performance Tennis Academy at the Sportscenter in Concord, North Carolina.

Coaching women to play tennis presents challenges quite different from those associated with teaching males. As a general rule, female matches involve longer points, more breaks of serve and less net play. Consequently, most tennis professionals and coaches focus their time improving forehand and backhand drives. Indeed, groundstrokes should be the foundation of a woman's game, but in my opinion and the opinions of many of my colleagues, backcourt play has been overemphasized.

The purpose of this article is to examine why this approach is, at best, shortsighted, and to present an alternative philosophy for coaching females - one that I believe produces far better players.

Let's first examine what females typically don't do so well.

1) The majority of women move slower forward and back than they do side to side.

2) Most women today do not volley well. This is especially evident when they're drawn to the net on their opponent's terms. Additionally, few seem to understand forecourt strategy.

3) Most women cannot slice well, nor can they effectively return a slice that is well hit to them.

4) Most females have weak second serves. Very few are able to hit a good kick second serve to their opponent's backhand.

Taking the above into consideration, my suggestions for training women and girls is as follows…

---

1. Teach female players how to slice groundstrokes. Train them how and when to use a 'floating' slice, and when to hit a 'driving' or 'knifing' slice. Developing these capabilities allow players to exploit the weakness of the western and semi-west-ern forehand grips (both are very poor grips for handling low, skidding shots).

Regrettably, these shots are not being taught today by the majority of teaching professionals. At the 2006 PTR Int'l Tennis Symposium, I attended one of the best presentations I have ever seen. It was titled Underspin Shots – The Underrated and Neglected Family of Strokes1 and it was given by Laury Hammel of the Longfellow Club.

During the clinic, Laury made the statement, "If you really want verification of the state of underspin in the tennis world, ask a typical tournament junior to rally with slice backhands."

Sadly, then, as now, they can't. Even the really good ones hit one or two and the third attempt usually results in a wild error.

2. From the earliest possible age, teach the drop shot and in the early stages, have students attempt it only from the service line (or closer) to the net. As skill improves, have students work on hitting drop shots from the baseline.

In a recent issue of Tennis magazine, Chris Evert commented on the fact that the females on the tour fail to use the drop shot enough. She wrote, "It's baffling to see women push their opponents five feet behind the baseline and never veer from pounding heavy groundstrokes. Mixing in drop shots is a smart play on two levels. First, women generally don't move forward as well as they do from side-to-side (the opposite seems true for men). Secondly, even if they do scramble up to get the ball, they're forced to approach the net - a place they don't like to be - on somebody else's terms."2

If the female pros aren't using the drop shot much (and I agree with Chris that they aren't), then there's little doubt that it's underused at the USTA, collegiate and high school levels of play.

3. From the earliest possible time, work on developing a mechanically sound service. If it is necessary, because of athletic limitations that a student use an eastern grip, as soon as practical, move them to a continental grip. Personally, I've had very few female students that I couldn't start out with a Continental grip.

A good service has three qualities: spin, speed and placement. Most females (who haven't put in adequate practice time) fail in at least one and usually two of these departments - particularly on the second serve (most often spin and placement).

Therefore, as soon as possible, develop a student's topspin or 'kick' serve. It is a fallacy that females are unable to learn a kick serve. There is absolutely nothing in the structure of a woman's shoulder girdle/shoulder complex that would prevent this! A few high profile coaches have suggested that strength limitations prevent women from developing this shot. This is simply not true. Females, pound for pound, can develop the same leg strength as a male. While this is not the case for upper body musculature - with proper tennis specific strength training females can develop very good relative upper body strength - strength which more than allows learning a good kick serve.

I have now taught competitive players for more than three decades and I have had numerous female students who could hit excellent top- spin serves. It's a matter of the coach placing a priority on the shot and having the skills to teach it! In a recent lecture, Dr. Ben Kibler identified a number of deficits exhibited in the service motions of many of today's female pros. These included: inadequate shoulder rotation away from the net on the backswing; overuse of the non-dominant leg (leg closest to the net at start of the service) in pushing upward to strike the ball; dominant hip (rotating toward the net) too soon - largely because of improper positioning of the feet prior to leg extension and an overuse of the stomach and trunk muscles in 'pulling' the racquet through the serve motion.3 Dr. Kibler cites these problems as casual factors in the recent increase in non-dominant leg injuries seen on the women's circuit. Frankly, I find it sad to see so many women - at all levels of the game - who only can hit a 'moderate slice' second serve. Let's face it, if you know your opponent can't kick the ball to your backhand, it sure is easy to attack that second serve!

---

4. From the first day on the court, coaches should spend each training session with mid court shots. Volley, half volley and overhead smash should be given priority along with ground- strokes. Once technique is sound, then students should be taught high percentage forecourt/mid court tactics and strategy.

All of this of this seems common sense to me and a great many of my professional colleagues. So why is it then, that women's play is so one-dimensional (i.e., all groundstrokes, mediocre serve) at all levels? My thesis is as follows: the older more 'seasoned' pros and coaches are retiring. They are being replaced by young, inexperienced pros, most of whom played a baseline game. These coaches never learned variety and they certainly didn't volley much. To be blunt, many of these young pros do not know how to teach these things. They could learn, but so few seem interested in bettering themselves, as evidenced by the attendance at both the USPTA and PTR symposia. Most of the teachers who attend these, and other workshops are older pros! There are exceptions of course, but for the most part, what I say is true. What we have then is limited experienced coaching propagating one-dimensional play. I've said it before in other articles I've written, but it's worth repeating - if all a player can do is hit forehand and backhand drives, then they have no way to win when their opponent is 15% (or more) better at hitting groundstrokes on that day. With sound slices, volleys, mid court skills and solid second (kick) serves, they have many ways to win!

What coaches of females today must do is to let their players (especially young juniors) know that learning a game with multiple shots, which involves constructing points, takes much more time to master than learning to compete with three shots (forehand drive, backhand drive, mediocre serve). A complete player will, in all probability, not be a Top 10 state ranked player in the 10s, 12s and possibly not in the early 14s. Once they reach the 16s however, they typically race past their ground- stroking only peers.

As a player matures, a coach should help them develop a style of play that is consistent with their athletic talents and the way they are psychologically 'wired'. If a girl's personality is such that she enjoys immediate reward, she is aggressive, athletic, and likes taking risks, then she should be coached toward being more of a net rushing player. If her personality is more artistic, she is creative, and she is moderately patient in receiving reward, then perhaps an all-court style of play would be a better fit. For a female who is extremely patient, with a proclivity toward low risk taking, who enjoys wearing down her opponents, then a baseline, grinding style would best work. I feel very strongly that most coaches of females overlook these factors and pigeonhole all their students into a baseline bashing style. Coaches in other sports don't take this approach - how silly would it be to insist that all batters on a baseball team be coached to be home run hitters?

I am fully convinced that if more pros would develop their students all court capabilities, American girls would land the majority of college scholarships (far more than today). Moreover, I think we'd see many more American players ranked among the world's elite professional players, not only in singles, but in doubles as well.

References

Hammel, Laury. "Underspin Shots – The Underrated and Neglected Family of Strokes." PTR International Tennis Symposium (2006).

Evert, Chris. "Game Changers." Chrissie's View/Tennis Magazine. March 2012. Pg.4.

Kibler, Ben. "Analysis of Male and Female Serve Motions: Differences, Similarities and Effect on Performance." Classroom presentation. PTR International Tennis Symposium, Feb. 24, 2012

Appendix V

Preventing Tennis Elbow

As published in Tennis Pro Magazine

January/February 2011

(Reformatted to Fit this Publication)

Preventing Tennis Elbow

An ounce of prevention is worth a pound of cure. This old adage holds true in many facetsof life, and it certainly applies to the painful scourge of the tennis player - tennis elbow.

by Jack Thompson

A PTR Master Professional, Jack has a gradu-ate background in Exercise Physiology and Motor Learning. During his 33 year career, he has worked as a head professional and was Head Men's and Women's Tennis Coach at Catawba College in Salisbury, North Carolina. Jack is co-author of Power, Speed and Stamina for Tennis: A Complete Guide for the Player andCoach. *An expanded second edition of the bookhe co-wrote with sport and orthopedic physicaltherapist, Gray Cook, was released in October 2010. A speaker at several PTR symposia, Jack is the Director of Tennis and Co-Founder (with Tim Wilkison) of the Salisbury Tennis Academy.*

Epicondylitis, or tennis elbow, manifests in three forms: lateral, medial and posterior. The most common type affecting tennis players is the lateral variety. It was first mentioned in English literature circa 1880, but unquestionably it occurred long before that, probably when our ancestors first used stone tools.

Regardless of the time of origin, lateral epicondylitis is a condition that has been largely misunderstood and oftentimes mistreated. Indeed, several medical articles in the mid-1960s contended that the injury rarely occurred in tennis players. This position gained little support at the time, however, and with the onset of the 1970s tennis boom, was proven incorrect. In fact, a study conducted among tennis players in 1972 (Nirschl, 1980), found that approximately 10 million adults over the age of 35 suffered from tennis elbow. This estimate did not include injury among the 10 million additional young adults and junior players who were participating in the sport during the 70s. While medical advances over the past several decades have resulted in more effective treatment and rehabilitation approaches, tennis elbow still remains a fairly common occurrence among players of all levels.

The primary cause of tennis elbow is the repetitive use of forearm flexors and extensors, which causes micro damage and partial tears near the musculotendinous junction (outside portion of the elbow), when the strain exceeds the strength of the tissues, and when the demand exceeds the repair process (Kisner and Colby, 1996). It stands to reason then, that the easiest means of preventing this condition is to ensure that adequate strength and flexibility is maintained in the forearm and wrist. Along these lines, I recommend and have always had great success using three primary exercises.

1. Rubber Band Finger Extensions

This exercise can be performed on a daily basis, virtually anywhere. Place one to three thick rubber bands around all five fingers of your playing hand *(Photo 1)*. Forcefully extend all five fingers outward *(Photo 2)*, making sure to keep the rubber bands centered over your middle knuckles at all times. Return your fingers to the original position, and you've performed one repetition. Repetitions should be performed quite rapidly with a workout consisting of three sets of 30-80 repetitions, with 30-45 seconds rest between sets. If you use a two-handed backhand, repeat the exercise with your non-dominant hand.

During my coaching days at Catawba College, I encouraged my players to wear rubber bands around their wrists.

Photo 1   Photo 2

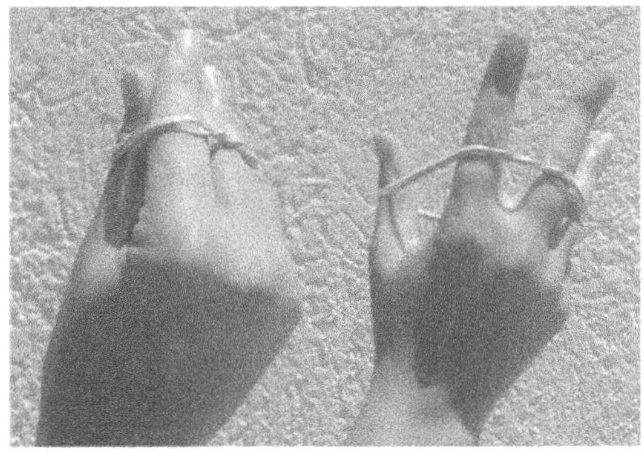

Whenever they thought about it, they could perform the exercise. To this day, it's a practice I follow, and since an initial occurrence of tennis elbow 15 years ago, I've never had another bout.

2. The Rice Bucket

The rice bucket is a highly effective means of strengthening the forearm and requires relatively little time. Use a medium size plastic bucket and fill it with rice to provide a resistance medium. Submerge your hitting hand to just past the wrist. Hold the lip of the bucket with your other hand to prevent the container from moving. Using your submerged hand and wrist only, make small circles in the rice for one minute, then reverse he directions of the circles for one minute. For a final minute, move your hand forward and back (wrist snap motion). The above describes one set. Complete two sets with two to three minutes rest between sets. Perform this exercise twice a week. If you are a two-handed player, be sure to exercise your non-dominant hand as well.

3. Powerball

The final exercise uses a Powerball (www.powerballs.com), a neat little wrist and forearm training device that has gained a great deal of popularity over the past six years (*Photo 3*). It is a handheld gyroscope that's encased in a clear plastic ball. Once started, the exerciser controls the tempo (resistance) by moving the hand and wrist in a small circle. The faster the circular motion, the more difficult the exercise.

I usually recommend 3.25 minutes at a moderate speed, ending with 45 seconds of high-speed work, for a total of workout of four minutes. As with the rubber band and rice bucket exercises, repeat with the non-dominant hand if you are a two-handed hitter. This exercise can be done daily, however, I feel four days a week, in combination with the other two exercises, is more than sufficient.

Try these exercises and I think you'll see that a little prevention goes a long way to enhancing your enjoyment and longevity in the game. You may even find that your tennis improves as a result of the strength gains to your wrist and forearm.

References
1. Kisner, Carolyn and Colby, Lynn. Therapeutic Exercise: Foundations and Techniques, 3rd ed.
2. F.A. Davis Co., 1915 Arch St., Philadelphia, pp 343, 1996.
3. Nirschl, Robert P. and Sobel, Janet. Arm Care: A Complete Guide to Prevention and Treatment of Tennis Elbow. Medical Sports Inc., Publications Division, Arlington, Va., 1996.
4. Nrischl, Robert P. Tennis Elbow: Prevention and Relief. Nautilus Magazine, pp 14-27, Summer, 1

Appendix VI

Sample Assistant Pro's Resume

As published in Tennis Pro Magazine

July/August 2014

(Reformatted to Fit this Publication)

Note: fictitious person

John Q. Tennis
215 Lake Shore Drive
Hampton, Va. 22321
jqtennis@yahoo.com
(980)-222-2222

Education

2006-2010 UNC Greensboro, Greensboro, NC
BS in Exercise & Sports Science
- QCA overall 3.1
- QCA in Major 3.3
2014 Certified (Professional), PTR

Professional Experience

2010- Present

Assistant Tennis Professional
- Aid in planning, marketing and teaching adults & juniors
- 10 and under specialist/programming
- Daily maintenance of clay court
- Pro shop supervision/sales

Playing Experience

- Ranked # 15 in Boys 18 singles in Southern Section 2005
- Won 11 NC USTA junior tournaments (Southern Section), 2005-2005
- Scholarship player, UNCG; played #3 singles and # 2 and #3 doubles 2006-2010

Awards Received

- All Conference Singles 2006, 2007, 2008
- Team Captain UNCG Men's Tennis team 2007, 2008

Other

- Coached 4 top 5 ranked adults (MATA) and 6 top 20 ranked juniors (MATA)
- Assisted in running Two River Fall Classic (L5), 2010, 2011, 2012, 2013, 2014,2015
- 2015 League Commissioner for Greater Peninsula Interclub League

<u>**References**</u>

Mr. Pete Smith
Director of Tennis
Two Rivers Country Club
Williamsburg, VA
pssmith@tworiversclub.org
(757)-555-5255

Mr. Bill Loeb
Men's Head Coach
UNC Greensboro, Greensboro, NC
bploeb@gmail.com
(336) – 221-0258

Ms. Penny Logan
Tennis Committee Chairman (2016)
Two Rivers Country Club
Williamsburg, VA
plogan@yahoo.com
(757)-926-2120

Appendix VII

We Still Need to Fix American Tennis

As published in Tennis Pro Magazine

November/December 2015

(Reformatted to Fit this Publication)

by Jack Thompson & Mark Allen
Co-Directors of the Performance Tennis Academy

PTR International Master Professional, and PTR Professional of the Year, Jack has a graduate background in Exercise Physiology and Motor Learning. During his 33-year career, he has worked as a Head Professional and was Head Men's and Women's Tennis Coach at Catawba College. He is currently Head Professional at Cabarrus Country Club in Concord and the Director of Tennis at the Old North State Club. Jack is co-author of Power, Speed and Stamina for Tennis: A Complete Guide for the Player and Coach.

Mark was Head Pro and Membership Director at Charlotte Racquet Club. He played DI tennis at the University of North Carolina at Charlotte. Mark finished 2010 as the #1 ranked Men's 4.5 Doubles player in NC and #3 ranked 5.0 Doubles player in the Southern Section. Also in 2010, he became Di- rector of Tennis at The Sportscenter in Concord, where he has grown his junior and adult programs more than 300%. Mark's company Performance Racquet Sports, manages the tennis programs at Cabarrus Country Club in Concord and Old North State Club in New London, both in North Carolina.

In 2012, I [Jack] wrote a three-part article published in *TennisPro* titled *How We Can Fix American Tennis*. This article sought to identify and offer solutions to the reasons the United States -since the mid-1990s - has been failing to produce international tennis champions. There were six reasons which were listed in order of importance as casual factors for the USA's demise. They were: 1) the decline in physical fitness of our youth, 2) the failure of our coaches to develop players with all court capabilities, 3) the fact that our juniors don't train enough on clay, 4) US coaches not teaching character, self-reliance, independence and how to recover from failure, 5) US tennis academies awarding too many scholarships to non-US students and 6) the overwhelming number of college coaches who recruit mainly international players.

Three years since the article was published, my colleague Mark Allen and I decided to examine whether progress has been made. Our investigation revealed the following

1. The Decline in the Physical Fitness of our Youth

We listened to many experienced coaches and tennis professionals give their opinions as to why we're failing to produce international champions and a recurring theme keeps coming up: that our best athletes are not choosing tennis as their primary sport. While this is true, we have found that the problem is far greater than this! In fact, we discovered that the US has far fewer good athletes available for all sports today as compared to years past – and the numbers prove it! Our research reveals:

- We studied the birth records from 1955 to 1963[4] (See Table 1). During this time there were 37,630,000 children born.

- We then surveyed 1973, when those born in 1955 would have been 18 and those born in 1963 would have been 10. Only 13%[5] of our youth ages 10-18 were obese or overweight in 1973. When we subtracted those kids who were obese or overweight (kids who probably

wouldn't play sports - and certainly not a running sport, like tennis), we were left with 32,739,000 children ages 10-18 who were viable candidates to play tennis/running sports in 1973.

When this same process was applied to births from 1996 to 2004 (Table 2), the total number born was close (roughly 1,640,000 fewer were born from 1996 to 2004) with a total of 35,990,000 born during these years. Here's the bad news, when we subtracted the obese/overweight kids (33% today), the total number of kids ages 10-18 available for tennis/running sports today is only 24,113,000!

The difference between these two snapshots in time: 8,626,000 fewer children ages 10-18 available for (running type) sports today as compared to 1973. To put this into proper perspective:

- 40 of our states have populations smaller than that!

- Virginia, our 12th largest state reported a 2012 population of 8,260,405, which is 365,594 people less than 8,626,000.

- According to current estimates, there are 163 countries on this planet with populations smaller than this. Only 93 have populations greater than 8.6 million!

When you further reduce today's athletic pool by subtracting the number of children playing soccer (5,000,000) and lacrosse (624,593), sports that didn't exist in the US in 1973, the difference is a staggering 14,250,593. Imagine if we had 14,000,000 more children in the athletic pool today and 8% (a number that's been reported as playing tennis today) chose tennis as their primary sport – that's 1,200,000 more tennis players ages 10-18! Or how about just 8,626,000 more? Eight percent of this figure is 690,080 (more tennis players ages 10-18)! With this increase, don't you think we could produce a few more Sampras and Everts?

So, how does the US compare with our foreign competition in terms of overweight/obese children? Very poorly! Today, as previously mentioned, a third (33%) of our school children are obese or overweight. Here's a rundown of what other countries have reported as their childhood obesity/overweight rates:

- Australia: 27% girls, 22% boys

- Germany: 17.6% girls, 22.6% boys

- Japan: only 3.5% of its entire population is obese/overweight

- China: 4.5% girls, 5.9% boys

- Russia: 25.7% boys and girls

- Canada: 26.1% girls, 28.9% boys

- Italy: 30.9% girls, 32.4% boys

- Spain: 22.9% girls, 32.9% boys

- United Kingdom: 26.6% girls, 22.7% boys

- France: 14.9% girls, 13.1% boys

- Romania: 25.4% boys and girls

- Switzerland: 13.2% girls, 16.7% boys

Only Argentina, Brazil and Mexico have a higher incidence of obesity among their children than the US, and they only exceed our totals by a percentage point or two.

To reiterate, saying that our best athletes are not choosing tennis is a gross understatement. Our main problem is that we have a far smaller athletic pool today than we have had in decades past. While it is true that many other countries focus more of their resources on tennis today, it is also true that a higher percentage of their kids are more fit to play tennis and other running sports. In addition, they also have fewer sports for their kids to choose from that could reduce their numbers participating in tennis.

Table 1

Births, Obese/Overweight Childrn (%) number of children ages 10-18 available for sports in 1973			
Birth Year	Total Births	Obesity 13% in 1973	# Children not obese in '73
1955	4,097,000	x .87 =	3,564,000
1956	4,218,000	x .87 =	3,670,000
1957	4,255,000	x .87 =	3,702,000
1958	4,245,000	x .87 =	3,693,000
1959	4,258,000	x .87 =	3,704,000
1960	4,268,000	x .87 =	3,713,000
1961	4,164,000	x .87 =	3,623,000
1962	4,098,000	x .87 =	3,565,000
1963	4,027,000	x .87 =	3,503,000
Total # of births 1955-1963 = 37,630,000		Total # of children ages 10-18 who were not obese* in 1973 - 32,739,000	

*Obese/Overweight

Table 2

Births, Obese/Overweight Children (%) number of children ages 10-18 available for sports in 2014			
Birth Year	Total Births	Obesity* 33% in 2014	# Children not obese* in '14
1996	3,899,000	x .67 =	2,612,000
1997	3,882,000	x .67 =	2,601,000
1998	3,942,000	x .67 =	2,641,000
1999	3,959,000	x .67 =	2,653,000
2000	4,059,000	x .67 =	2,720,000
2001	4,026,000	x .67 =	2,697,000
2002	4,021,000	x .67 =	2,694,000
2003	4,090,000	x .67 =	2,740,000
2004	4,112,000	x .67 =	2,755,000
Total # of births 1996-2004 = 35,990,000		Total # of children ages 10-18 who were not obese* in 2014 = 24,113,000	

* Obese/Overweight

1973 total 32,739,000 - 2014 total 24,113,000
= 8,626,000 more children available for running type sports in 1973

The Relationship Between Obesity/Overweight Percentages in US Children and US Men's and Women's World Tennis Rankings

In order to determine the relationship between the childhood obesity rate (10–18-year-old boys and girls) in the US and the decline in US men's and women's world tennis rankings, a simple correlation of data was performed. (See Table 3).

A correlation is a statistical measure that indicates the extent to which two or more variables (in this case obesity/overweight % and US tennis world rankings) are related. A positive correlation indicates the extent to which those variables increase or decrease in parallel; a negative correlation reflects the degree to which one variable increases and the other decreases. Correlation coefficients can range from 0 (no relationship) to 1 (a perfect relationship). A high correlation (or strong relationship) would be considered .7 and above.

Table 3

Year	% obese 10-18 year olds	US men in Top 100	US women in Top 100
	Incidence of childhood obesity/overweight in US and ATP/WTA world rankings of US players 1978-2014		
1978	13%	35	50
1979	13%	31	51
1980	13%	36	52
1981	13%	39	51
1982	13%	41	48
1983	13%	38	48
1984	16%	41	42
1985	17%	34	42
1986	17%	31	37
1987	18%	25	43
1988	20%	28	34
1989	21%	28	23
1991	21%	29	25
1991	21%	17	23
1992	21.5%	17	23
1993	22%	14	22
1994	22.5%	18	20
1995	24%	6	13
1996	26%	14	16
1997	27%	9	14
1998	29%	8	14
1999	29%	11	14
2000	30%	8	14
2001	31%	6	15
2002	32%	10	12
2003	33%	10	10
2004	33%	10	13
2005	33%	8	10
2006	33%	8	9
2007	33%	6	10
2008	33%	6	4
2009	33%	5	4
2010	33%	5	7
2011	33%	6	5
2012	33%	8	9
2013	33%	7	9
2014	33%	7	10

**Obese/Overweight*

When the data was analyzed, we found:

There is an extremely strong negative correlation between the percentage of overweight US 10–18-year-olds and the number of men in the Top 100 tennis rankings (r35) = -.934, p<.001, as well as women (r35) = -.957, p<.001. In other words, as obesity/overweight percentages increased rankings dropped. In fact, it wasn't far off from being a perfect correlation for both men and women!

It should be noted, however, that a high correlation does not necessarily prove causation, but in this case, it does show an extremely strong relationship! Here's a good example of two variables having a strong positive relationship, but no causal relationship. Consumption of ice cream in the summer (variable 1) and summer drowning deaths (variable 2). Both increase dramatically in summer (positive relationship). Eating ice cream, however, does not cause people to drown. A third mitigating situation - hot weather - is the causal factor tying these two variables together.

Another, stronger statistically, method of examining 'change' over time was then performed by classifying the data according to decades. Specifically, an ANOVA test, followed with post-hoc Tukey test was performed. This resulted in the following (See Table 4).

Obesity changes significantly over these three decades, $F(2,34) = 177.01$, MSE = .001, p<.001, ηp^2=.91 (very strong effect), with the 70/80s (M=15.60%) showing far fewer obese 10–18-year-olds than the 1990s (M=24.1%), which in turn showed fewer obese children than did the years since (M = 32.60%). Leaving out the numbers, you can say that obesity percentages have increased significantly over the past 37 years, classified by decade.

Number of US men in the tennis Top 100 rankings changed significantly over these three decades, $F(2,34) = 111.95$, MSE = 21.78, $p<.001$, $\eta p^2=.87$ strong effect), with the 70/80s (M = 33.92) showing far more US men in that elite group than the 1990s (M = 14.30) and the decade-plus since (M = 7.40). Leaving out the numbers, you can clearly see that the percentage of top US men has decreased over these years.

Number of US women in the tennis Top 100 rankings changed significantly over these three decades, $F(2,34) = 113.88$, MSE = 35.03, $p<.001$, $\eta p^2=.87$ (very strong effect), with the 70/80s (M = 43.42) showing far more US women in that elite group than the 1990s (M = 8.50) and the decade-plus since (M = 9.40). Leaving out the numbers, you can clearly see that the percentage of top US women has decreased over these years.

With the lack of men and women in the Top 100 today comes a secondary problem - kids just can't identify with any champions - and this lessens the likelihood of choosing tennis as a primary sport. They used to have Ashe, Connors, Smith, McEnroe, Chang, Agassi, Sampras, Courier, King, Evert, Davenport and Austin. Ask any American child today (one who doesn't follow tennis) who John Isner is, and they couldn't tell you. They sure wouldn't know who our third best male player (Steve Johnson, #51 in the world)

is. In fact, most tennis fans wouldn't know who he is.

We do believe that these data are one of the factors, and in all probability, one of the top two reasons that has led to our demise. The other five points in this article also have played a significant negative role.

Table 4

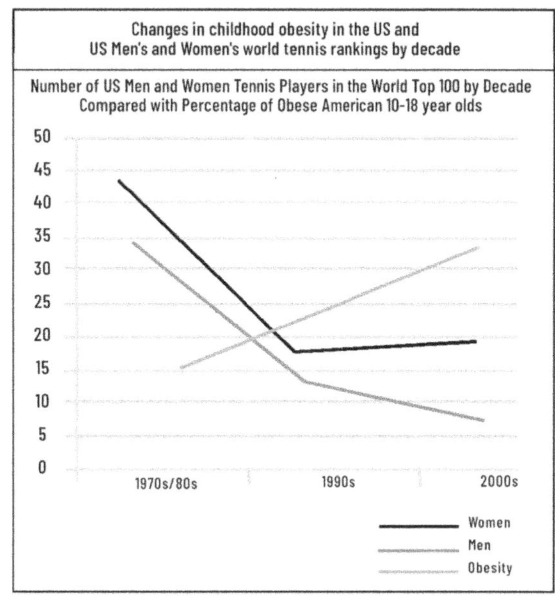

The Solution

As stated in How We Can Fix American Tennis, we believe that Physical Education (nationwide) must return to a sound program of strength training and conditioning, much like we had in the 1960s and 70s. Physical Education should be mandatory K-12 and funded accordingly. Current and past research clearly shows that those children (and adults) who exercise regularly far outperform their sedentary counterparts on both physical and cognitive tasks. Children should have to 'dress out' and when the teacher instructs them to run, they should run (at their own pace), or suffer the consequences. This isn't happening in a majority of physical education classes offered today. Students should have to shower after physical activity; it's a part of learning good hygiene!

The upper body strength of our youth today is extremely disappointing - 65% of boys and girls in 1995 ages 12-17 (the last time meaningful data was collected nationwide) could only do 0-1 pullup. We feel sure it's just as bad and probably worse today. Children today just do not climb, wrestle, play on monkey bars and throw things (e.g. snowballs, dirt clods, etc.) like their 50s, 60s 70s and 80s counterparts did. Much of their time today is spent indoors gaming. In fact, a 2012 PBS interview with the Director of the National Gaming Institute revealed that by the time a kid today reaches 21, they have gamed more than 10,000 hours, which is equivalent to the number of hours they spend in the middle school and high school classroom combined! To improve our children's upper body strength, the rope climb, weighted clubs, medicine balls, kettle bells and the pegboard should be put back into Physical Education classes.

We have talked to a number of coaches and physical educators who have placed the blame for America's weight problem on the fact that high fructose corn syrup (HFCS) is so prevalent in foods today. Apparently, they have based their opinions on the 2004 study (Bray et.al.)6 that contended that HFCS is a direct causative factor for obesity. This is clearly not the case. John S. White (2008)[7]

conclusively showed that HFCS is not the unique cause of overweight/obese children and adults in the USA or elsewhere.

School lunches can be made more healthy, and it's admirable that our first lady, Michelle Obama has brought light on this issue, but without vigorous daily physical activity, our numbers of obese/overweight children will continue to soar. Indeed, a recent PBS radio report predicted that by 2025, 50% of our youth will be obese or overweight! The President's Challenge (formerly known as the President's Physical Fitness Awards Program) should be reinstated in all school districts. These tests should be given (as they used to be) at the beginning and end of each school year.

Understand, I say these things from the perspective of a physical educator, my undergraduate degree is in Physical Education. I taught Health and Physical Education in the middle school from 1976-1981. Mark and I strongly believe that when these measures are implemented, we'll begin to see improvement, but it will take time.

2. Failure to Develop a Full Court Game & Too Much Drilling with Too Little Play

In the US, we still seem stuck on the notion that everyone needs to play as either an attacking baseliner or a counterpunching baseliner. Throughout the country, we see the majority of pros feeding endless hoppers of balls at academies and promoting a 'grip it and rip it' philosophy of competing. Understand that we use the term 'academy' to include any large junior group training that occurs at virtually all clubs around the country. At most sessions that we visited, the time spent on the court broke down to something like this: 75-80% groundstroke training (drives only); 10-15% service work and 5-10% mid-court and net play.

In 2000, my good friend and colleague, PTR Pro and former ATP tour player, Tim Wilkison stated in NC Tennis Today, "The juniors today cannot volley well, cannot hit a slice well or return a slice that's well hit to them." Fifteen years later, this is still the case!

So what we're seeing at virtually all levels of junior play today in the US is a power baseline game. It is as if teaching pros were trying to coach US players to beat the Europeans and South Americans at their own game! This approach is wrong and here's why - training everyone to play the same way is inconsistent with how humans are wired psychologically. Any sports psychologist would agree with this! Do we train all our football players to be quarterbacks? How about training all our baseball players to be home run hitters or train all our track team runners only for the 800 meters? In tennis, a kid who likes immediate reward, is risk taking, athletic and wants to volley, would best be served by being coached as a net rusher. Those juniors who are more patient, like the grind of long points and enjoy wearing down an opponent, would be better coached as a counterpunching or perhaps attacking baseliner. An artistic or creative child, who is a problem solver, is probably best served by being taught an all-court game Perhaps the best summation of how limiting a ground game only style can be was stated in a recent conversation with Tim Wilkison (who currently coaches several tour players from China). He said, "If all you can do is hit hard ground strokes, and your opponent is 8-10% better that day at it than you, you lose. There can be no back up strategic plan if you don't have other shots!"

The Solution

In the 2012 articles I wrote and now, we contend that coaches should teach students (from an early age) all the shots! (PTR is currently doing this in our new pathway.) This includes slices, topspin drives, flat drives, flat serve, slice serve, topspin serve, backhand overhead, half volley, volley, dropshots, etc. By age 12, a child should be able to demonstrate each of these shots. This does not mean that they can necessarily execute all of them successfully in match play. Coaches employing this training philosophy would, of course, need to counsel students (and their parents) that learning a complete game takes much more time than learning to just bash topspin forehands and backhands.

Students who are training in this manner typically annihilate their groundstroking only peers by age 16 or 17. The reasons should be obvious - a player who has a complete game is able to compete if s/he is losing by adjusting strategy. For instance, if one is losing at the baseline with drives, s/he could slice or perhaps purposely hit short (drop shots) to bring the opponent forward and follow up with passing shots or lobs. If that didn't work, a complete player could try rushing the net. Having multiple shots is essential in being able to build points.

Please coaches, we implore you to switch gears and teach a full court game and then help your players find a game style that works for them! The cookie cutter approach of the past 20 years has failed - and failed miserably! Just look at the stats. In 1983, we had 39 men and 51 women ranked in the Top 100. Today we have only 7 men and 10 women!

Finally, coaches in the US need to have their players drill less and play more! At our academy, we insist that our juniors play at least two practice matches per week. Incidentally, we don't consider tournaments practice matches. A practice match involves the student calling or texting someone to set up a time and place to play a best 2 out of 3 set match. Across the US today, this is not happening. Kids will play if it's arranged for them by the pro. This wasn't the way it was in the 70s, 80s and early 90s.

In the September/October 2014 issue of TennisPro, PTR International Master Professional Jorge Capestany[8] stated, "Today's junior players are not playing enough sets. I am fortunate enough to travel the world as a speaker and coach, and everywhere I go, American coaches tell me they have the same problem. Kids take drills (group lessons), private lessons, special events, but avoid match play like the plague. In my own program, I have seen the shift as well. When I taught players in the 1980s, they couldn't wait to get out on the court and play sets. Drilling was only one part of their overall training regimen, and it comprised two to four hours a week at the most. Back then, the good players additionally took a private lesson and played tournaments on the weekend, or if there were no tournaments, they played practice sets." Later in the article, Jorge summarizes with, "The end result is the development of an army of American kids who can strike the ball beautifully but cannot seem to win a match. If the game is the best teacher, then match play is best for the game."

3. Failure to Practice and Compete on Clay Courts

There is no evidence to suggest that US junior players have devoted more practice time on clay courts over the last three years. There may be a few more clay court tournaments overall, but this doesn't constitute practice.

The Solution

US pros and coaches must demand that their students train and play more practice matches on clay. For more information on this subject, refer to How We Can Fix American Tennis - Part 2.[2]

4. Failure To Teach Character, Self-Reliance, Independence, Overcoming Adversity & How to Rebound From Failure

We have seen no improvement in this area. Regrettably, as a country, we have grown weak. The rugged individualism, strong character and strong work ethic that used to define Americans has been replaced by the notion that if you fail, the system is unfair, and you're 'entitled' to some measure of success. It's certainly occurring at an unprecedented rate at the federal level, but it's also happening in sports! Don't think so? What about giving every kid a trophy? What about not keeping score? How about eliminating MVP (most valuable player) or the giving of such an award to a senior whose record falls far short of an underclassman?

In a recent article[9], Dr. Allen Fox commented on this situation. Specifically, he examined the role that modern psychologists have played in America's decline. He states, "Before psychologists became the accepted arbiters of proper American behavior, these issues* [family rules, adult purpose, resolve, reliability, integrity and character] were determined by trial and error and centuries of experience. Ideas of education, child rearing, character development, etc., were passed on from person to person verbally and by example. Familial traditions were taught to children by parents, grandparents, other relatives and family friends and associates. These ideas, well tested in practice, came from personal, close-by resources, not theories originated at a distance. Among these ideas were the likes of children should be seen and not heard, spanking is a reasonable punishment for disrespecting and/or disobeying parents, rote learning is a necessary part of early education, negative reinforcement is useful for delineating boundaries, self-esteem comes from successful accomplishments, high standards of altruism, morality and conduct must be established for children by parents and other adults in authority, etc."

*author's insert

Dr. Fox, who has a Ph.D in Psychology from UCLA and taught Psychology at Pepperdine University, goes on to say,

""Psychologists changed all of this. Beginning in the middle of the last century psychologists, with the help of the mass media - radio, television, and magazines - began to quickly and widely disseminate their half-baked new ideas. These untested assertions had a powerful impact on the lay public, gaining extraordinary credibility because they were stated by psychologists and because they appeared on television and radio, now the accepted purveyors of celebrity status. In short, hundreds of years of trial-and-error tested ideas were discarded in favor of sweet-sounding theories - unproven - but given undue weight because people with P.h.Ds after their names got together with the mass media."

Later in the article, Dr. Fox states, "Fixing the educational system attracted special attention* (of which sports is a part) with a new bias toward making learning fun rather than driving students to do the necessary but difficult. Rote learning of multiplication tables seemed old fashioned compared with new math. Children needed to be stimulated in school with modern gadgets, fancy projects and hanging mobiles, rather than coerced with traditional memorization of correct spelling and grammar, driven by blackboards, books, pencils, papers and bad grades for the inept. It sounded timely to state that 'children are people too' and that their ideas, although they may only be 10 years old, must be seriously considered.

Youngsters should, for example, have a say at the breakfast table, but also in their school curriculum, rather than having this determined by fuddy-duddy educators. Even more importantly, their self-esteem had to at all costs be kept elevated, so corrections to their work had to be done with great tact and grades elevated lest weaker students by psychically damaged (Dr. Spock had proclaimed that there should be 10 positive reinforcements for every negative one, a 'fact' that he pulled out of his left ear). And 'modern' educators were repelled by the risk to youthful self-esteem posed by competition of any kind, tempting some to propose that sporting events dispense with keeping score and that school grades be done away with altogether."

Is it any wonder, then, why the US is floundering (both in education and tennis)? Concurrent with the steady rise in liberal child rearing practices since the 1980s has come a strong sense of entitlement to excellence… and when students fail, they are ill equipped to handle the emotions that accompanies failure. With a 'specialist' coach for every aspect of their development, many of today's junior tennis players are counseled, coddled, provided answers to situational (on court and off) dilemma's they should have been allowed to figure out on their own, and told by their parents that "you failed because the situation was unfair." The majority of kids today are simply not resilient in the face of adversity. Teaching pros, especially the young ones, are terrified to dwell on character, self-reliance, independence, integrity, honesty and how to recover from failure, for fear of losing students to the guy up the road who's all about just hitting balls. In fact, it is a disturbing recent US trend that students jump ship and go to another coach if they disagree with the coach or fail to gain immediate success. In many cases, we see parents using multiple coaches - which doesn't work, especially in the early stages of learning - in the hopes that one provides the 'magic' performance cure. This goes on and on, eventually resulting in the child being totally confused as to how to play.

We have no hard data to prove it, and it may be impossible to find such data, but we suspect that juniors from other countries aren't spoon fed by their coaches and parents as are our kids. I've been a PTR member since 1981, and I can honestly say that I've met very few parents of international players (and I've met many), who were anything less than highly supportive of their kid's tennis coach. I was Head Men's and Women's Tennis Coach at Catawba College (DII) from 1998-2004, and I often heard the following comment made by Division I, II and III coaches (and I'm paraphrasing here), "I love recruiting the international players. They're tough, they're not spoiled, they're highly coachable, and the parents aren't intrusive in the coaching process!"

The Solution

There was a time when the majority of US kids possessed strong character, were tough, self-reliant, independent, respectful, coachable, and able to rebound following failure. Unless we re- turn to teaching these values to all of our youth, we don't see anything more than random success for US tennis. Let's face it - kids are kids - it's the adults in this country who have changed!

5.Tennis Academies and the Awarding of International Scholarships

We only have anecdotal evidence, but it's strong anecdotal evidence. Conversations with parents and pros around the country suggest that many…far too many, tennis academy scholarships are being given to international players. Illustrating this are the comments of Michael Burton, whose son Jared plays at the highest USTA level of competition in Texas. In a letter to the editor of Tennis magazine he states, "Listening to the commentary of the predictable McEnroe brothers during the US Open about how the future of men's tennis in America looks bright sounded a tad hypocritical to me. The problem with American junior tennis is not that there is not enough talent in the United States; the problem is that former tennis pros and US junior development officials go outside America to recruit talent.

"Just look at tennis pro Kei Nishikori, who was brought to America from Japan to train at the Nick Bolletieri Academy in Florida when he was 14. Despite the talent right here in the US, tennis academies are recruiting players outside North America to develop their tennis skills on the pro tour. American universities typically recruit junior players outside America as well - for example, South African tennis player Kevin Anderson, who played for the University of Illinois.

"The problem with 'American tennis' is not that there is a lack of talent here - it's that our top tennis facilities and top college tennis programs deliberately go outside the continent to recruit male players. In light of this fact, I think Tennis magazine could have chosen another feature for Generation Next featuring American junior boys - Stefan Kozlov was born and raised in Macedonia."

While it is true that student success helps increase long term academy revenues, why can't US tennis academies give the scholarships to mainly US players? Wouldn't having successful US players do just as much, if not more to build academy prestige? It's baffling to see so many international juniors 'riding in the apple cart' while US families pull it (with their finances)!

The Solution

The media and perhaps the USTA could be helpful in this regard, but essentially tennis academy owners and directors must adopt a philosophy of America First. We understand that they're running businesses, but feel just as much, if not more, income could be realized by awarding the majority of scholarships to US children.

6. US College Tennis & the Recruitment of International Players

Unfortunately, nothing has changed since 2012. In fact, this practice may be even more common. Today, nearly half of all NCAA tennis players are from countries other than the US.[11] The top 25 Division I teams in Men's and Women's tennis list 175 players from abroad - some 37% of all players. Among the top 25 women's teams in Division I, approximately 40% of scholarships go to international players. The top 25 women's teams in Division II award roughly 70% of their scholarships to internationals.[11]

It should be obvious why this hurts American tennis. Internationals take spots on teams those American players could have. American families need the financial aid and college tennis is an important step for those good enough to go on to the pro tour. Yet in roughly 50% of cases on a men's and women's team (DI, DII), we are funding a non-US citizen's development!

The Solution

As a collective force (NCAA, USTA, parents, pros, athletic directors at universities, etc.), we should demand that college coaches invest in American players! If the NCAA chose to act, it could impose legislation restricting each team to two internationals. This would allow international recruitment and give the majority of opportunity to our citizens.

Several brave pros and college coaches have spoken out

- Wayne Bryan, father of the #1 ATP ranked doubles team of Bob and Mike Bryan, Luke Jensen, former ATP pro and Head Women's Tennis Coach at Syracuse University, and Tina Tharp, Head Coach at West Chester University - in sup- port of recruiting American players. College coaches must do their part to stop bringing in players who are using the college experience to train for the pro tour. We've heard from several tennis fans and authorities that, "if the coach recruits Americans and starts losing, he'll be fired!" We think that in the overwhelming majority of cases this just isn't so. Tennis, at every college, is a non-revenue sport. We believe that if a coach told his athletic director, "I want to do my part to build tennis in the US, and expand our alumni base by recruiting American players, players who have good grades, are good citizens and who really want to attend our school" that the AD's response would be supportive of getting back to the way it was.

Another comment we have heard is, "if we only recruit American players… there wouldn't be enough players to go around to fill the squad rosters." Really? We don't remember schools unable to field teams before international recruitment became prevalent. It might be that the depth of squads would be affected, but this would be the case with all schools across the board!

Come on college coaches - Put America First!

Summary

No one factor by itself has been the unique cause of the USA's demise in international tennis. It has been the synergistic effect of all of the aforementioned reasons that has been and continues eroding our chances of success. Until there is a serious effort to address and improve these problems, we believe that the United States will only show random (and very little if any) long term success in international tennis. Coaching (and playing) any sport is a pragmatic venture - what you're doing either works or doesn't work. What we've been doing for the past 15-20 years has resulted in rapid and complete failure! The solutions are at our fingertips - we need only to use common sense and act!

References

1. Thompson, Jack (2013). "How We Can Fix American Tennis: Part I." TennisPro (May/June) pp 24-27.

2. Thompson, Jack (2012). "How We Can Fix American Tennis: Part II." TennisPro (July/Aug.) pp 11-12.

3. Thompson, Jack (2012). " How We Can Fix American Tennis: Part III." TennisPro (Sept./Oct.) 00pp 19-21.

4. "Births and Birth Rates in the United States Between 1910 and 2005." www.infoplease.com/ipaA0922289.html

5. Bishop, Middendorf, Babin and Tilson (2005). "Childhood Obesity." ASPE Research Brief. Aape.hhs.gov/health/reports/child obesity/index.cfm.

6. Bray, GA, Nielsen SJ, Popkin, BMV (2004). "Consumption of High Fructose Corn Syrup in Nutrition. Vol. 79, pp 537-543.

7. White, John S. (2008). The American Journal of Clinical Nutrition. "Straight Talk about High Fructose Corn Syrup: What it is and What it Ain't." Dec.2008. Vol 88, no. 6 17165-17215

8. Capestany, Jorge. (2014). "Serial Drillers: How Group Lesson Programs are Killing American Junior Tennis." TennisPro (Sept/Oct.) pp 7-9.

9. Fox, Allen (1996). Excerpts from Book Proposal: "How Psychologists Have Been a Disaster to the United States."

10. Corbett, Melissa Lawrence (2013). "Why is American Tennis Dying?" Team Stream Bleacher Report Inc.

11. The Sports Digest: The United States Sports Academy ISSN: 558-6448.